THERE'S ALWAYS ROOM FOR CHOCOLATE

THERE'S ALWAYS ROOM FOR CHOCOLATE

Recipes *from* The Chocolate Room

Naomi Josepher, Jon Payson + Georgia Freedman

with Executive Pastry Chef Carmine Arroyo

Photographs by Ben Fink

Illustrations by Elizabeth Ashley

RIZZOLI
NEW YORK

New York · Paris · London · Milan

To Clare and Mac, our sunshine, and to our parents,
for encouraging us to explore.

★

First published in the United States of America in 2016
by Rizzoli International Publications, Inc.
300 Park Avenue South, New York, NY 10010
www.rizzoliusa.com

★

★

★

2016 2017 2018 2019 / 10 9 8 7 6 5 4 3 2 1

★

Designed by Jennifer S. Muller

★

Distributed in the U.S. trade by Random House, New York
Printed in China
ISBN-13: 978-0-8478-4863-8
Library of Congress Control Number: 2016939611

Contents

Recipes by Time Commitment

When diving into the recipes in this book, it's helpful to know which recipes can be whipped up quickly and which recipes will take a little extra time and work.

**Weekend Projects: Multi-Part Desserts Best
Made Over the Course of Two or Three Days**

Our Story

In many ways, The Chocolate Room started the day we met in 1993 while working together at a restaurant in Manhattan. Jon was a drummer in a rock band, performing in downtown clubs. Naomi was a modern dancer, performing with independent choreographers. As young artists, we didn't have the means to go out for a lot of dinner dates, so we developed our own ritual: we went out for dessert. As we ate our way through our favorite dessert destinations, we would daydream about opening a dessert café. It would be a cozy place where people could come to relax and indulge in something extraordinary; a place people could visit several times a week, but special enough to be a location to celebrate milestones; a place that felt very accessible, and at the same time, totally indulgent; a place you could walk into and not feel guilty asking, "Can we just have dessert?" At the time, it was just a fleeting thought. We had come to New York City to immerse ourselves in our art, so we stayed focused on our pursuits.

In 2002, we moved to Park Slope, a quiet Brooklyn neighborhood full of tree-lined streets and hundred-year-old brownstones. Where Manhattan had been grand and imposing, Park Slope felt like a small-town neighborhood. It was also the beginning of a movement of innovative people opening businesses on a budding Fifth Avenue. While walking our dog, we met many local business owners, and in our daily chats, we realized we had much in common with them: similar talents, work ethic, and entrepreneurial spirit. So why couldn't we rent a space and develop our own business? Without making a conscious decision, we started looking around for a suitable location for our café or shop. Whenever we saw an empty storefront, we'd pop in to inquire about rent.

At first, we envisioned a dessert café, since Park Slope had nothing of this sort. We felt it could fill a void for people like ourselves who wanted a fun place to visit with friends to share a special dessert and a glass of wine. But our path narrowed and deepened when Jon was inspired by a book, *The New Taste of Chocolate: A Cultural and Natural History of Cacao with Recipes* by Maricel Presilla. He became intrigued and passionate about chocolate. There was something about the history and discovery of the plant, the alchemy of turning something that grows on a tree into one of the world's most treasured ingredients, and the artistry of turning that ingredient into something extraordinary to eat that captured his imagination. He called Naomi with an idea: What if we open a chocolate shop?

We found a dilapidated space directly across from our apartment that was miraculously just within the price we could afford. Rents were starting to increase with the demand, so we felt fortunate to find a landlord offering us a fair rent. We signed a lease, emptied our savings accounts, and went to work on renovations, spending our nights tearing out drywall, chipping away plaster, exposing brick, and installing tiles.

Although our initial intent was to open a traditional chocolate shop that offered bars and confections, the more we discussed—and lived in—the space, the more ambitious we became. The space felt just large enough to function as a café. We brainstormed the idea of a dessert café centered around chocolate. We went to business research libraries to find out just how much Americans liked chocolate, and if the demographics of the surrounding Brooklyn neighborhoods would support this business idea. In addition to building, we spent the next six months writing a business plan and raising money.

In creating our menu, we chose to focus on simple, classic chocolate desserts that we loved. Jon's favorite dessert is a hot fudge sundae, so we developed a hot fudge sauce that stays thick when poured on our homemade ice cream, yet is chewy as it cools. Jon also had strong childhood memories of chocolate pudding, so we created a grown-up version with dark chocolate. And since we were calling ourselves The Chocolate Room, we needed to make the best chocolate layer cake we'd ever tasted.

The Chocolate Room opened the last week of January 2005. Jon could be found in the front of our shop at the espresso machine, steaming milk for serving after serving of hot cocoa, blending together milk, sugar, cocoa powder, and chunks of milk chocolate, releasing a decadent aroma. Naomi was in the back of our intimate and cozy café, serving thick slices of our chocolate layer cake, pudding topped with whipped cream, and chocolate fondue with homemade marshmallows. Already people were introducing themselves to us, telling their stories and asking for ours. Already we were adding something to the neighborhood: chocolate was bringing joy and a new sense of community. We looked up from our work, and then at each other that first Saturday afternoon of business. The café was bustling. There was a line snaking out the door. It hit us: we had actually done it. The idea that had been born eighteen months earlier, to open a café dedicated to chocolate, was working.

In the years since, we've had amazing experiences. We feel so grateful for our incredible staff, both past and present, and a community that has cared about us and cheered us on since the day our door opened. We've had unbelievably generous investors and friends who have offered us time and talents to help us grow. We've been lucky enough to be featured in magazines and publications that have offered us wonderful press like *O Magazine*, the *New York Times*, the Food Network, and the Cooking Channel. And we've expanded by opening a second shop a few miles away in Cobble Hill.

In addition, we've had a succession of wonderful pastry chefs, each of whom has brought his or her own personality and talents to the job. Our current executive pastry chef, Carmine Arroyo, has been with us since 2012. He has become an integral part of our success. Carmine's talents and his impeccable sense of flavor have expanded our menu and introduced us and our guests to new, inventive desserts with ingenious twists on some of our old favorites. The high standards that he encourages from our staff, and models himself, have helped us expand our production. His sense of fun in the kitchen keeps us, and our staff, energized.

There's Always Room for Chocolate allows us to share a little bit of the warmth, comfort, and delight that make The Chocolate Room a special place. We hope you enjoy these recipes as much as we've enjoyed creating them. We've had a lot of fun over the years watching the smiles these desserts have brought to so many faces.

—Naomi Josepher and Jon Payson

Chocolate: An Introduction

There is something magical about the cacao tree. Tall and thin, it branches out to form a wide canopy of emerald-green leaves that shade what may be the most miraculous-looking fruit of all time—huge gold, ruby, and magenta pods that grow straight out from the tree's trunk and all its branches like enormous, bright ornaments. To the first person who stumbled upon a cacao tree, it must have looked like it was placed in the ground by the hands of the gods.

Cacao was probably first domesticated by the Olmec, an ancient people who lived in the coastal areas of the Gulf of Mexico from roughly 1200 BCE to 400 BCE, and who built the first great civilization in Mesoamerica. The Olmec left no records of how they used their cacao, but the Maya, who established their civilization in that same region six centuries later, made cacao into hot and cold drinks, some of which were flavored with ingredients like honey, vanilla, achiote (the seeds of the annatto tree), or chiles, and some of which were mixed with masa or ingredients that produced foamy tops on the drinks. They also cooked with cacao, using it as a flavoring for foods like fish and turkey.

To the Maya, however, cacao wasn't just a cooking ingredient. Many of their myths treat cacao as a sacred food that nourished the gods, and it was an integral part of religious and burial ceremonies. Toward the end of the Mayan period, cacao formed the basis for a thriving trade network that ran all the way from the southern part of the Gulf of Mexico down to the Gulf of Honduras and made the last of the Mayan communities tremendously wealthy. And as the Mayan civilization disappeared, their last kingdoms fought wars over control of the best cacao-growing areas.

In the fourteenth century CE, when the Aztecs conquered much of Mesoamerica, they subjugated many of the Mayan cacao-growing regions and established trade with others. They used cacao to make a wide variety of cold drinks similar to those the Maya drank, and these drinks and the cacao pods themselves were also used in religious rituals as symbols for blood and for the human heart. By the time the Spanish reached the area in 1519, cacao had become so important that it was used as currency, and only the elite were allowed to drink it.

The Spanish noted the importance of cacao almost as soon as they arrived in the New World, and they, too, began to drink chocolate, though they preferred it hot and flavored it with sugar and spices like cinnamon. In the seventeenth century, chocolate became a popular beverage in noble households throughout Spain, and from there it was exported across the rest of Europe. People from England to Italy became obsessed with drinking chocolate, and "chocolate houses," similar to today's coffee houses, became popular. In the late seventeenth century, cooks in Italy and France also began to use chocolate to make desserts like custards, cakes, mousses, and ice creams, and some Italian cooks even experimented with adding it to savory dishes.

The most radical change in how chocolate was prepared came in 1828, when a Dutch chemist named Coenraad van Houten developed a process for separating the cacao butter from the rest of the bean in order to produce a finer cocoa powder that dissolved better in liquid. The excess cocoa butter from this process could then be added to regular ground chocolate to produce a smoother, thinner chocolate mixture (now called couverture) that could be molded into elaborate shapes. The invention of couverture made it possible for chocolatiers to develop treats like truffles and candy bars and, ultimately, led to the creation of all the chocolate-based treats that are now wildly popular around the world.

Bean to Bar

All cacao beans go through a series of complex processes on their way to becoming chocolate:

The cacao fruit and seeds are scooped out of their pods, placed in covered boxes or other receptacles, and left to ferment in their own pulp for a number of days.

After fermenting, the cocoa beans are spread out and left to dry in the sun or in covered sheds, or, in some cases, are dried over a fire.

Once dry, the beans are shipped to chocolate manufacturers, where they are roasted, and the shells and cocoa nibs (the meat of the beans) are separated.

The nibs are ground to create cocoa liquor, a thick paste of melted cocoa butter and coarse cocoa particles. This mixture can be pressed to extract much of the cocoa butter (in which case, the remaining cocoa mass can be further processed to make cocoa powder), or it can be used as is to make unsweetened chocolate.

If the cocoa liquor will be used to make a finished chocolate bar or confection, it is often mixed with additional cocoa butter and sugar, flavorings, and/or dairy (for milk chocolate) and then further refined to make a paste. This processing can be done by passing the chocolate through rollers, putting it in a ball mill (which presses the chocolate against ball bearings), using a melanger (which presses the chocolate through two stone wheels), or using a number of other tools.

The mixture is then put into conching machines that agitate it continuously for many hours or days to remove some of the moisture, distribute the cocoa butter evenly, develop the overall flavor, and create a smooth, creamy texture.

The chocolate is then tempered—heated and cooled carefully at specific temperatures so that the chocolate crystals align properly—to give the finished chocolate a shiny surface and a crisp snap.

Types of Cacao

All chocolate is made from the fruit of *Theobroma cacao*, a tropical evergreen tree native to Central and South America. Over the years, this species has evolved (and been bred) into three distinct varieties:

Criollo

This variety is grown primarily in Central America, and it produces the most flavorful, nuanced, and aromatic cacao beans. Criollo is also, however, the most difficult type of cacao to grow. The trees are smaller and produce fewer pods than other types of cacao trees, and they are also susceptible to disease, so the variety accounts for only 1% of all the chocolate produced worldwide.

Forastero

This variety of cacao is grown everywhere from South America to West Africa to Southeast Asia. Its trees are much more prolific than the Criollo, producing an abundance of large pods, but their seeds produce chocolate with a less nuanced, more bitter flavor.

Trinitario

This variety is a hybrid of Criollo and Forastero that combines some of the best qualities of both. The trees were first cross-bred in Trinidad in the late eighteenth century, and the resulting variety is now grown all around the world and is the cacao that is used by most high-end chocolate makers.

What Chocolate Do We Use?

At The Chocolate Room, we use a handful of wonderful, high-quality chocolates for our baked goods, desserts, and confections. These chocolates give our treats their phenomenal flavors and wonderful textures.

Belcolade

This Belgian-made chocolate is the basis for most desserts at The Chocolate Room. Belcolade sources their cacao from all over the world and blends it together to achieve a consistent flavor and texture for all their products. We use the company's Noir Absolu Ebony 99.5% chocolate, Noir Supreme 70%, Noir Superior 60%, and Noir Selection 55%. Belcolade doesn't sell their chocolate directly to the public, but it can be purchased online through third-party vendors.

Valrhona

All our cocoa-based desserts are made with Valrhona's 100% cocoa powder. It is a Dutch-processed cocoa, which means it has been alkalized to lower its acidity and give it a darker color and smoother flavor. We also use the company's Ivoire 35% white chocolate, Jivara 40% milk chocolate, and Manjari 64% dark chocolate for some of our specialty desserts. Valrhona chocolates can be purchased on the company's website and are also available at many specialty stores.

Guittard

We use chocolate from this California-based company for many of our milk chocolate and white chocolate desserts. The company, which was started by a Frenchman, Etienne Guittard, during the Gold Rush, sources their cacao from small family farms all over the world. We use the company's Soleil d'Or 38% milk chocolate and Crème Francais 31% white chocolate, which are available through their professional line and can be purchased through their website and at many specialty food stores.

Arriba Gold

This single-origin chocolate from Ecuador is another of our favorites. It is made using the Arriba varietal of cacao, which is known for its complex flavor and aroma and does not contain vanilla or any other added flavors. We use Arriba Gold 70% chocolate in our flourless chocolate cake, and we also sell a line of The Chocolate Room chocolate bars made from Arriba Gold chocolate. The company also makes a white chocolate, a 55% chocolate, an 80% chocolate, and a 100% chocolate. Their products can be purchased through their website.

In addition to these standbys, we have also made wonderful desserts and confections using other brands of chocolate, and in our shops we sell bars from Mast Brothers, ki'Xocolatl, Pacari, Madécasse, and other brands we love. Over the years, however, we've discovered that different chocolates will produce different textures in our desserts. Flourless chocolate cake and brownies (both recipes with lots of melted chocolate in their batters) are particularly sensitive to the type of chocolate used: with some chocolates they become denser, and with others, they become lighter. We suggest that you play with these recipes a little bit to see how your favorite chocolate affects them. In the end, after testing our recipes with lots of different kinds of chocolate, we're confident that no matter what brand of chocolate you use, the results will be totally delicious!

Chocolate Chip Almond Cake
recipe on page 32

Tools

Basic Tools and Equipment

Ovens

At The Chocolate Room, we use convection ovens to bake all our cakes and baked goods. But this technology is too new and expensive for most home kitchens, and we've found that different companies' convection ovens bake differently; in fact, the two different sizes of commercial convection ovens in our two different locations bake items so differently that we use different baking temperatures at each café. So all the recipes in this book have been reformulated (and tested!) for baking in a conventional home oven. In some cases, this means we've increased some leavening ingredients to help baked goods rise the way they do in our convection ovens. In other cases, we found that the home version of our desserts have a slightly different texture than the ones baked in the cafés—for instance, some of the cookies spread a little more in a conventional oven.

Stand Mixers

We've found that the consistent mixing action of a stand mixer is essential for getting the right texture in our cakes and baked goods. We use large Globe mixers in our kitchens, but the recipes in this book have been scaled down and tested in a standard KitchenAid mixer. If you have to use a hand mixer instead of a stand mixer, make sure that you're beating all the ingredients evenly (not leaving unmixed clumps on the sides or bottom of the bowl), and pay attention to the texture of your batter—you should focus on making the batter look right, not on following the beating times called for in the recipes. See "How to Whip up Butter, Cream & Eggs" (page 64) for descriptions of what different ingredients look like when they're mixed properly.

Scales

In our café kitchens, we almost always measure our ingredients on scales. For the recipes in this book, we have converted most of our measurements to cups, tablespoons, and teaspoons, but for ingredients that can't be measured this way, like chocolate, we've kept the measurements in ounces and pounds. Kitchen scales are fairly easy to come by, but when we buy scales, we choose postal scales, designed for weighing mail. They're cheaper and larger than kitchen scales and are just as reliable. We particularly like the MyWeigh UltraShip digital scale: the display can be set in ounces, pounds, or grams, and the display can be detached from the scale so you can see it even if you're weighing ingredients in a very large bowl.

Candy Thermometers

A good candy thermometer—one that can read temperatures as high as 392°F (200°C)—is essential for tempering chocolate, making caramel, cooking sugar syrup for mousses and fudges, and many other cooking tasks. At The Chocolate Room, we always use digital thermometers because they're much more accurate and easier to read than nondigital thermometers. You can also set them to sound an alarm when your sugar syrup or caramel reaches the desired temperature. When buying a candy thermometer, make sure you get one that clips to the side of the pot or bowl; if you have to hold the thermometer with your hand, it's easy to burn yourself with hot steam or sugar. We particularly like Maverick brand thermometers because they are designed for very hot temperatures and their displays can be separated from the temperature probes. When using a digital thermometer, remember that you need to keep the electric components dry and that you'll want to have extra batteries on hand.

Sheet Pans

When buying sheet pans (also called cookie sheets or baking sheets), we always choose the kinds with 1-inch-tall sides. These are much more versatile than any other kind of sheet pans because they hold on to nonstick silicone liners better, can have cooling racks set directly into them, and won't warp. Most important, they can also be used to make our brownies and marshmallows. When buying sheet pans, look for 13 x 18-inch pans; if you're buying them through a professional kitchen supply site, they'll be called "half sheet pans."

Wire Pan Grates

Instead of using small cooling racks for our cookies and cakes, we buy wire pan grates, which are essentially cooling racks that fit snugly inside a sheet pan. These grates have nice small square openings, so cookies and little chocolates don't slide through them, and because they fit into sheet pans, you can glaze cakes on them; the excess glaze will fall through and collect in the pan. When buying pan grates, make sure you get the size that will fit in your sheet pans.

Cake Pans

We make cakes of all sizes, from tiny 6-inch-diameter checkerboard cakes to 10-inch-diameter layer cakes, but all our cake pans have one thing in common: 3-inch-tall sides. This makes the pans much deeper than most cake pans, and that allows us the flexibility to make tall cakes, like our Chocolate Chip Almond Cake (page 32), or to make thick layers that can

be cut in half horizontally, like the layers for our Checkerboard Cake (page 43). You'll want to have one 10-inch round pan, three 9-inch round pans, one 8-inch round pan, and three 6-inch round pans if you plan to try all the cakes in this book.

Springform Cake Pans

Springform cake pans, which have sides that detach from the pan's bottom, are essential tools for making cheesecakes and mousse cakes, which are too delicate to unmold from regular cake pans. When buying springform pans, make sure to get pans with the deepest sides you can find. At The Chocolate Room, we use pans with 3-inch sides, but most of our recipes will work in 2½-inch-deep pans, too. You'll need an 8-inch pan and a 9-inch pan for the recipes in this book.

Pie Tins

The pie recipes in this book are designed to fit into 9- and 10-inch ceramic or glass (Pyrex) pie plates. You can also make all of our pies using metal pie tins, but the crusts may bake more quickly than indicated in the recipes. At The Chocolate Room, we also use disposable aluminum pie tins for our pies (see "How to Bake the Perfect Chocolate Pie Crust," page 90).

Muffin Pans

When buying muffin pans for making cupcakes, make sure to get the kind made from light-colored aluminum rather than darker nonstick pans; the darker metal actually holds heat differently and will cause the sides of the cupcakes to brown too much. We use "standard" muffin tins, which are about 3 inches in diameter and 1 inch deep.

Ramekins

Many of our custards and puddings are made in ceramic ramekins. They fit into standard-size ramekins that hold 5 ounces of batter and are 3⅛ inches in diameter. These ceramic ramekins are ideal for egg-based custards because they help them bake gently and evenly. When we make Sticky Date Pudding (page 118) or Spiced Molten Chocolate Cakes (page 59), however, we use disposable aluminum ramekins of the same size because they're easier to push on and peel back when it's time to unmold the cakes.

Silicone Liners and Parchment Paper

At The Chocolate Room, we use both silicone liners and parchment paper. We usually use silicone liners (Silpat brand) for baking cookies because they're reusable and have a slightly textured surface that keeps cookies and caramels from sticking to them.

We use parchment paper for lining cake pans and loaf pans because we can cut it to exactly the size we want. We use a lot of parchment paper, so we buy the kind that is already cut into large sheets from specialty baking stores; it sits flatter than the kind that comes on rolls and is therefore easier for us to work with.

Plastic Mixing Bowls

While most home cooks use ceramic or metal mixing bowls, we always use sturdy, heat-resistant plastic mixing bowls, like the kind made by Cambro labeled as "pebbled salad bowls." These bowls are much sturdier than ceramic bowls, and they're perfect for tempering chocolate because they can be put in the microwave but cool relatively quickly (see "How to Temper Chocolate—A Few Simple Methods," page 126).

Rubber Spatulas

We use rubber spatulas for everything from scraping the sides of mixing bowls to stirring tempering chocolate. The best rubber spatulas are very sturdy and heatproof and have long plastic handles so that you don't have to stick your hand into hot pots. (Spatulas with wooden handles are less useful because they can hold moisture, which can cause mold growth or ruin tempering chocolate.) It's best to buy rubber spatulas that don't have detachable handles because

the joint where a detachable handle meets the spatula can hold water, and that can ruin tempering chocolate.

Whisks

We use two different styles of whisks: strong, sturdy whisks that won't bend in thick batter (like the batter for our brownies), and thinner, lighter whisks that will bend when pressed on the side of a bowl so that they can scrape the sides effectively. The best all-purpose whisks are narrow, stainless-steel "French" whisks, though if you want to whip cream by hand, you should also have a rounder "balloon" whisk.

Large Strainers

We use heavy-duty metal strainers to remove overcooked bits of egg from ice cream and custard bases and to remove flavorings like vanilla beans or coconut flakes from heavy cream.

In the cafés we particularly like to use cone-shaped "China cap" strainers because they are very sturdy and easy to set inside large plastic containers. Mesh strainers work well too, but they should be sturdy enough that you can press on them firmly without worrying that the mesh will separate from the frame or that any part of the strainer will get bent.

Piping Bags

We use piping bags for all sorts of things (see "Using a Pastry Bag" page 108), so we always like to have more than one ready to go. At the shop we use Patisse brand 2-inch heatproof disposable pastry bags, which can be used with or without a metal pastry tip. For home cooks, we suggest getting at least two large reusable cloth or silicone pastry bags—that way you won't have to wash and dry one right away if you need to pipe two different kinds of frosting or batter.

Other Helpful Tools

Immersion Blender

We use a large immersion blender to blend spices into our hot cocoas, smooth out the texture of frosting, and blend ingredients for everything from our strawberry sauce to our blackout cake filling. An immersion blender is much more efficient than a countertop blender because it can be used to blend ingredients while they're still hot and doesn't have a blender canister that requires scraping. When buying an immersion blender, look for one with a blade that can be detached from the base so that you don't get water on the electrical elements when you're washing it. We particularly like De'Longhi TriBlade blenders because they have a lot of power and can handle stiff mixtures.

Ice Cream Scoops/Cookie Scoops

We use a number of ice cream scoops and cookie scoops in our kitchens because they make portioning batter for cupcakes and dough for cookies easy and consistent. We use a 2½-ounce (2¼-inch-diameter) ice cream scoop for cupcake batter, a 1½-ounce (1¾-inch-diameter) cookie scoop for cookies and macaroons, a ¾-ounce (1½-inch-diameter) scoop for almond clusters, and a ½-ounce (1-inch-diameter) scoop for mini macaroons, caramel for caramel turtles, peanut butter fudge for peanut butter cups, and the chocolate syrup that sits at the bottom of our Black-Bottom Butterscotch Custard (page 113).

Offset Spatulas

Offset spatulas—long, flat, flexible spatulas with handles that are "offset" from (i.e., raised above) the plane of the spatula—are standard tools in any pastry chef's kitchen, and they can also be incredibly helpful for home cooks. The offset handles are particularly helpful because they keep you from dragging your hands in the batter/frosting or scraping your knuckles on the sides of sheet pans. Small (4¼-inch) offset spatulas are helpful for smoothing filling onto cakes, testing chocolate to see if it is tempered properly, and separating baked cookies from parchment paper. Large (8-inch) offset spatulas are great for frosting cakes, spreading brownie batter, and smoothing out the tops of cheesecakes. We buy Ateco spatulas, which are nice and flexible, and Dexter-Russell or LamsonSharp spatulas, which are a little stiffer and therefore better for stiff frostings and batters.

Paintbrush/Pastry Brush

We've found that traditional silicone pastry brushes don't hold enough water to be very effective, so when we need pastry brushes, we buy a few small (1 to 1½-inch-wide), high-quality paintbrushes. They're perfect for brushing simple syrup onto cakes, buttering cake pans, and cleaning sugar crystals off the insides of pots of caramel. Any brand of paintbrush will work as long as it's high enough quality that the bristles won't come off the brush while you're working with it.

Metal Ruler

We use rulers for any number of jobs—measuring the height of cakes, the size of brownies, the amount of sauce in a pot, etc. We prefer long, sturdy, metal rulers (rather than wood or plastic) because we can immerse them in liquid, their edges don't rub down over time, and their markings don't rub off or fade.

Deep Hotel Pans

Deep-sided metal "hotel" pans—the kind of pans you see holding food at restaurant buffets—are perfect for making water baths for cooking custards, flourless cakes, and cheesecakes. They function like deep casserole dishes or roasting pans, but they have metal lips along the edges that are ideal for securing aluminum foil over the tops of the pans. In our kitchens we always have 2-inch-deep pans for flourless cakes and custards and 4-inch-deep pans for making water baths for tall cakes. For home kitchens, half-size "half-hotel pans" (which measure 10⅜ x 12¾ inches) are more likely to fit into conventional ovens and refrigerators than the full-size versions.

Metal Storage Containers

In The Chocolate Room kitchens, we use a variety of metal storage containers—we have tall, round "bain" containers and rectangular "third pans" with lids, which can be stacked on top of each other. These metal containers are essential for holding hot sauces, caramels, ice cream bases, and anything else that needs to be poured into a heatproof container. The bains (short for "bain-marie," the French term for a water bath) are ideal for sauces because you can put them directly into hot water to warm them up, and the third pans are great for storing ice cream because they stay cold for a while when they're removed from the freezer.

Plastic Storage Containers

We use two different kinds of plastic storage containers. The first are cheap, disposable, quart- and pint-size containers, the kind you get when you order soup at a Chinese takeout restaurant. These are fantastic for storing frostings and glazes and they also hold stacks of cookies nicely. The second are heavy-duty Cambro containers. These have measurement lines on them so you can see how much of a particular ingredient you have and have heavy-duty snap-on lids. We buy big 8-quart containers to store cake batter and smaller 4-quart containers for cookie dough.

Bench Scraper

A metal bench scraper—a flat, metal tool used by pastry chefs for getting dough off the counter (or "bench")—has multiple uses. It's perfect for dividing up chunks of dough, cutting butter into cubes, folding delicate dough (like the chocolate dough for our strawberry shortcakes), and scraping excess chocolate off polycarbonate chocolate molds.

Kitchen Torch

We use a kitchen torch for many things. They're great for traditional tasks like caramelizing the tops of crème brûlée or browning sugar on bananas for our banana split, but they're also useful for breaking up bubbles on the tops of custards before they go into the oven, melting sugar syrup that has stuck to the side of a mixing bowl, heating the sides of springform pans before unmolding chilled cakes, and making chocolate ganache shiny after it has been refrigerated. When buying a kitchen torch, we recommend getting a small propane torch at a hardware store instead of buying a kitchen-specific torch. The replacement canisters of propane are easier to find, and the torch attachment is nice and sturdy. We particularly like the BernzOmatic TS4000-Trigger-Start Torch because it has a nice strong flame and a safety lock.

Plastic Squeeze Bottles

We store most of our sauces in clear, reusable plastic squeeze bottles. This lets us portion out the perfect amount of sauce for our drinks and sundaes, squeeze them onto cookies to make s'mores or into ramekins for black-bottom butterscotch custards, and use them to decorate plates.

Masking Tape and Permanent Markers

We label everything at The Chocolate Room, and we suggest you do the same. We keep big rolls of masking tape and a handful of permanent markers in the kitchens—this way we're never guessing about when something was made or how much batter or base is in any given storage container.

Specialty Tools

Polycarbonate Chocolate Molds

Stiff molds made from polycarbonate plastic are an essential tool for making chocolate—these molds are how we make chocolate shells for our peanut butter cups, chocolate chess pieces, chocolate hearts, or any other molded chocolate treats. We prefer clear molds, which let us see the bottoms of the molds (to check for air bubbles), rather than opaque molds. For the recipes in this book, the only mold you'll need is the one for peanut butter cups, which is called a "fluted round mold"; the indentations in the mold should be about 1½ inches in diameter.

Flexible Silicone Molds

Flexible molds made from heat- and cold-proof food-grade silicone are built for shaping ingredients like caramel that would be hard to remove from a stiff polycarbonate mold; once the caramels are set, you can pop them out of the mold by pressing on the backs. For the recipes in this book, the only mold you'll need is the one for the chocolate caramel turtles, which is a half-sphere mold with 10-ml indentations, about 1½ inches in diameter.

Ateco Round Cutters

Round Ateco brand cutters are circles of stainless steel that allow you to cut perfectly uniform biscuits for strawberry shortcakes and cookie dough for chocolate-and-cream sandwich cookies. We also use them to cut out the bull's-eye pattern necessary to make our Checkerboard Cake (page 43). The cutters come in sets of eleven or twelve nested circles that range from 7/8 inch to 4 7/16 inches.

French Sauce Gun

This candymaking tool is essentially a funnel with a mechanism that lets you open and close the bottom by simply squeezing a handle. As the name indicates, these "guns" can be used to dispense sauces, but they're particularly helpful for portioning hot caramel into molds (like the molds for our caramel turtles) without burning yourself.

Turntable Cake Decorating Stands

All professional bakers use cake decorating stands that have rotating tops; this allows you to hold a spatula still and rotate the cake itself, which gives you a smooth, even layer of frosting. We prefer Ateco cake stands because they have a sturdy metal base that lifts the cake a full 6 inches off the counter (to help us see the whole thing clearly) and a removable rotating top that is easy to clean.

Cardboard Cake Circles

Whenever we frost cakes, we put the cakes onto cardboard cake circles so we can transfer the cakes from the decorating stand to a box or serving stand. Even if you're not using a decorating stand, it's helpful to use a cake circle so that you can decorate the cake on a cutting board or another plate and keep the serving plate clean.

Whipped Cream Dispenser

Whenever we put whipped cream on top of a drink or an ice cream sundae, we use a whipped cream dispenser that uses nitrous oxide to dispense the cream through a star-shaped tip.

Our Favorite Sources

We use many different sources for purchasing our baking pans, chocolate-making equipment, and hard-to-find ingredients. Here are a few of our favorite stores and websites:

Kerekes Bakery & Restaurant Equipment Inc.
bakedeco.com
6103 15th Avenue
Brooklyn, NY 11219
800 525 5556

JB Prince
Tools, baking supplies, and restaurant equipment
jbprince.com
36 East 31st Street
New York, NY 10016
800 473 0577

New York Cake and Bake
Baking and candy-making supplies
nycake.com
56 West 22nd Street
New York, NY 10010
212 675 CAKE

Broadway Panhandler
Commercial-grade cooking tools for home cooks
broadwaypanhandler.com
65 East 8th Street
New York, NY 10003
866 266 5927

Chefs' Warehouse
Specialty ingredients and gourmet foods
chefswarehouse.com
718 842 8700

Spiced Molten Chocolate Cakes

recipe on page 59

cakes

How to Assemble and Frost a Perfect, Showstopping Cake

Home cooks often find that their cakes fall apart when they're assembled, frosted, or cut into slices. So why don't our towering chocolate cakes have the same problem? Here are a few techniques that will ensure perfect, beautiful, stable cakes every time.

Chill the cake

Refrigerating or freezing the individual layers of cake helps the cake solidify so it won't crumble and fall apart when you cut into it. Chilling the layers until just before you're ready to frost the cake also helps them stay intact when you pick them up and move them around, and keeps them firm so you don't end up with crumbs in the frosting. Once the cake's layers have been stacked with frosting between them, the whole thing should be wrapped in plastic wrap and refrigerated again so that the frosting will firm up and hold the cake together.

Cut the domed tops off the cake layers to create flat surfaces

It may seem like a waste to cut a slab off the top of each cake layer, especially if the dome is ¼ inch thick or taller, but having nice flat tops and bottoms on all your layers will keep the cake stable when you assemble it. (The excess cake can be turned into a delicious snack for the cook.)

Cutting layers in half

If you have to cut cake layers in half (to make thinner layers), don't just cut straight through, or you'll end up with uneven layers. Instead, score the cake all the way around at the halfway point. Cut 2 to 3 inches into the cake on one side, following the score marks, then turn the cake about 20 degrees and cut into it 2 to 3 inches again. Repeat the process, turning the cake and cutting in just a little with each turn, until you've cut through all the edges and only have to cut through the middle of the cake.

Turn the middle and top layers of the cake upside down

To make sure your cake has a nice flat top with even edges, turn the middle and top layers upside down when you assemble your cake. If you've already trimmed the domes off the layers, they'll sit very comfortably without wobbling.

Moisten the cake

To keep the cake moist, brush each layer with a generous amount of simple syrup. If you want to add a little extra flavor to the cake, you can add a flavorful liquid to the syrup; for instance, a lemon cake tastes lovely with some extra lemon juice added to the syrup, and a chocolate cake can be augmented by the addition of a raspberry or orange liqueur. Once you've added the syrup, let the cake sit for a few minutes to absorb the liquid before continuing with the recipe. (If you've cut the tops off the layers, the syrup will absorb better.)

Applying Frosting

Here's how we make sure frosting covers a cake evenly and fills in any gaps between the layers:

 Put the prepared frosting into a pastry bag or a large zip-top bag and cut open the tip so that you have a ½-inch opening. Pipe a thick ring of frosting along the seams of the cake, lifting up the edges of the cake to pipe between the layers if there are any gaps or if any parts of the cake are sagging and need to be propped up.

 Pipe a thick spiral of frosting onto the top of the cake, and pipe rings along the sides, using up most of the frosting. (There will be gaps where the cake shows through the rings of frosting.)

 Using a large offset spatula, a wide flat knife, or a stiff rubber spatula, spread the frosting evenly along the top of the cake, letting the excess fall off onto the sides. Once the top of the cake is even, smooth out the frosting on the sides of the cake, filling in any bare spots with the remaining frosting in the pastry bag.

 If the frosting becomes too stiff as you work, you can immerse the spatula in a container of very hot water and then wipe it dry. This will heat the spatula enough to help the frosting spread easily. Repeat as necessary.

 When the cake is evenly frosted, take one last pass with the spatula along the sides of the cake to create a little bit of a raised edge of frosting along the top corners of the cake. Use a wet paper towel to clean up any excess frosting that is smudged along the bottom edge of the cake.

The easiest way to achieve a smooth, evenly frosted cake is to work with a movable turntable. This allows you to maintain an even distance between the cake and your spatula: simply hold the spatula still, in one place, and as you turn the cake, the spatula will smooth the frosting out until it's evenly distributed around the cake. (Make sure to hold the flat edge of the spatula against the frosting, rather than an angled edge, or the spatula will remove frosting as the cake spins.) You can use the same technique with a non-moving cake plate by simply turning the plate, but it won't be quite as easy or as even.

Chocolate Layer Cake

Makes one 9-inch three-layer cake

This was the very first recipe we created for The Chocolate Room. We decided that if we wanted to open a restaurant dedicated to chocolate, we needed to serve the best chocolate cake we had ever tasted. Our first chef, Margaret Kyle, tested every classic American chocolate cake possible, and every few days we'd meet at our apartment to try the results, gathering around the kitchen table to taste and refine our ideas. Was the cake moist enough? Was the flavor rich enough? Did the whole thing slide off the fork just so? It took weeks of experimenting, but one day Margaret presented us with the most perfect cake we'd ever had. With three towering layers of rich, moist cake, a thick filling of blackout pudding, and creamy frosting—which together boast three different kinds of chocolate—the cake was a showstopper.

Make all the components at least one day before you're going to serve this cake so it stays firm and doesn't fall apart when sliced (see Make Ahead, page 29).

Chocolate Cake

5 extra-large eggs, at room temperature

2 teaspoons pure vanilla extract

1 cup unsweetened Dutch-process cocoa powder

3 cups cake flour

1 tablespoon baking soda

½ teaspoon kosher salt

1 cup plus 2 tablespoons (2¼ sticks) unsalted butter, at room temperature, plus extra for greasing the pan

3½ cups dark brown sugar

1½ cups sour cream

1½ cups cold coffee or water

Blackout Cake Filling

¼ cup cornstarch

2 tablespoons plus 1 cup water

1¼ cups granulated sugar

2 tablespoons light corn syrup

½ cup unsweetened Dutch-process cocoa powder

5 tablespoons unsalted butter, cut into small pieces

¼ teaspoon pure vanilla extract

To Assemble

½ cup granulated sugar

½ cup water

Chocolate Frosting (page 31)

Chocolate-covered espresso beans and cocoa nibs (optional)

recipe continues on the next page

Make the Cake

1. Preheat the oven to 350°F. Cut circles of parchment paper to fit the bottoms of three 9-inch round cake pans. Lightly butter the pans, line them with the parchment circles, and butter the parchment.

2. In a small bowl, whisk together the eggs and vanilla. Sift the cocoa powder into another small bowl, breaking up any chunks. Sift together the cake flour, baking soda, and salt into a large bowl.

3. In the bowl of a stand mixer fitted with the paddle attachment, cream the butter and brown sugar on medium speed for 3 minutes, until the mixture is very light and fluffy. Add the egg mixture and continue mixing on medium-low until the mixture just comes together, about 30 seconds. Stop the mixer and scrape down the sides and bottom of the bowl to incorporate any unmixed ingredients, then beat on medium for 30 seconds more, until there are no lumps or unmixed ingredients.

4. Add the cocoa powder and beat on low until incorporated, covering the bowl with the plastic guard or a towel to keep the cocoa from flying out of the mixer.

5. Add one-third of the flour mixture and mix on low until just combined. Stop the mixer, scrape down the sides and bottom of the bowl, and add half the sour cream. Mix on low until just incorporated, about 30 seconds, then stop the mixer and scrape down the sides and bottom. Repeat with another third of the dry ingredients and the remaining sour cream, scraping down the bowl after each addition. Add the remaining flour mixture, mix until just incorporated, and scrape down the bowl again.

6. With the mixer running on low, pour the coffee into the batter in a thin stream, then mix on low until the batter is uniform, about 20 seconds.

7. Remove the bowl from the mixer and finish mixing by hand, using a rubber spatula in a beating motion and scraping the sides and bottom of the bowl to ensure that all the ingredients are evenly incorporated and that the batter is completely smooth and lump-free.

8. Divide the batter evenly among the prepared pans. Bake the cakes for 45 to 50 minutes, until they spring back when pressed lightly with your fingers and a paring knife inserted into the center of each cake comes out clean. Let the cakes cool to room temperature, then remove them from the pans, pull off the parchment paper, wrap each layer of cake in two layers of plastic wrap, and put them in the refrigerator or freezer to chill.

Make the Filling

1. In a small bowl, mix together the cornstarch and 2 tablespoons of the water; set aside.

2. In a small saucepan, combine the remaining 1 cup water, the sugar, and the corn syrup. Use a wet paper towel to wipe down the sides of the pot and have a cup of water with a pastry brush nearby. Bring the mixture to a vigorous boil over high heat. If sugar crystals form on the sides of the pan, brush them down with the wet pastry brush. Add the cocoa, whisk it in, and allow the mixture to return to a boil. Reduce the heat to medium-low to keep the mixture from bubbling over.

3. Add 3 tablespoons of the cocoa mixture to the cornstarch mixture to warm it up. Whisk the cornstarch mixture to make sure it isn't adhering to the bottom of the bowl, then add it the pan with the rest of the cocoa mixture. Bring the mixture to a boil over medium-high heat and cook, whisking continuously and scraping the bottom of the pot, until it becomes thick and puddinglike.

4. Remove the pot from the heat and whisk in the butter and vanilla. Use an immersion blender to make sure the filling is smooth and there are no remaining pockets of cocoa. (Alternatively, you can wait for the pudding to cool, then blend it in a blender.) Set the filling aside to cool with a piece of plastic wrap pressed against its surface to prevent a skin from forming. When the filling has cooled to room temperature, transfer it to an airtight container and refrigerate until very cold.

Assemble the Cake

1. Combine the sugar and water in a small saucepan and heat over medium heat, stirring occasionally, until the sugar has dissolved; set the simple syrup aside.

2. Remove the cake layers from the refrigerator or freezer. If they're frozen, let them sit for 5 to 10 minutes. With a bread knife, cut the dome and any raised edges off each cake layer, taking off as much as necessary to create a flat, even surface.

3. Set one layer on a cake stand or flat plate. With a pastry brush, coat the top of the cake with ¼ cup of simple syrup and let it soak in for a minute. Top the cake layer with about half the blackout pudding, spreading it evenly and leaving a ½-inch border bare around the edge of the cake. Take a second cake layer, turn it upside down, and set it on top of the filling. Brush more simple syrup onto this layer and top it with the remaining filling. Top the filling with the last cake layer, placing it upside down, and brush on more simple syrup. Wrap the entire cake in two layers of plastic wrap and set it in the fridge to firm up for at least 4 hours or, ideally, overnight.

4. Unwrap the cake and apply the chocolate frosting evenly over the top and sides. (See page 24 for our favorite frosting technique.) If you like, you can decorate the top of the cake with little clusters of chocolate-covered espresso beans and cocoa nibs. ★

Make Ahead

Because we make this cake in large batches, every element is designed to be kept in the refrigerator or freezer for at least 5 days without damaging the flavor or texture in any way. The baked cake layers can wrapped in two layers of plastic wrap and refrigerated for up to 5 days or frozen for up to 1 month. The pudding will keep in the refrigerator for up to 5 days. The assembled, unfrosted cake can be wrapped in plastic and kept in the refrigerator for up to 4 days or in the freezer for up to 1 week. The frosted cake will keep in the refrigerator for 3 to 4 days.

Alternate Version
Single Layer of Chocolate Cake

Our chocolate cake is also used as a component in other desserts, like our Turtle Cheesecake (page 47) and Chocolate Mousse Cake (page 61). You can either make a full batch of the batter and use the excess to make cupcakes (see below), or you can use these ingredient quantities to make a single layer:

2 extra-large eggs, at room temperature

½ teaspoon pure vanilla extract

⅓ cup unsweetened Dutch-process cocoa powder

1 cup cake flour

1 teaspoon baking soda

¼ teaspoon kosher salt

6 tablespoons (¾ stick) unsalted butter, at room temperature, plus extra for greasing the pan

1 cup dark brown sugar

⅓ cup sour cream

½ cup cold coffee or water

Prepare the batter as directed on page 28, being extra vigilant about scraping down the sides and bottom of the bowl as you mix the ingredients together to make sure that everything gets incorporated. Bake as directed. ★

Above and Beyond
Chocolate Cupcakes

One batch of batter will make about 46 cupcakes. Preheat the oven to 350°F. Line muffin tins with paper liners. Fill each cup with about ¼ cup batter (we use an ice cream scoop to portion the batter so that the cupcakes are even—and because it's the least messy way to fill the cups). Bake for 20 minutes. Frost with 2 recipes' worth of Chocolate Frosting (page 31), using a pastry bag fitted with a star tip or a butter knife or small offset spatula. ★

Chocolate Frosting

Makes 1 quart

This frosting was developed for our Chocolate Layer Cake (page 27). But we think it's the best frosting we've ever tasted, so we use it on many of our cakes, including our German Chocolate Cake (page 39) and Boston Cream Pie (page 103). It's built on a base of cooked eggs, which gives it a rich, creamy texture, and it has both 60% and 100% chocolate, which gives it a rich flavor and very smooth texture.

6 ounces dark chocolate (preferably 60% cacao), coarsely chopped

3½ ounces unsweetened chocolate (preferably 100% cacao), coarsely chopped

¾ cup plus 2 tablespoons (1¾ sticks) unsalted butter

5 extra-large eggs

1 cup granulated sugar

½ cup water

¼ teaspoon salt

Special Tool

Digital candy thermometer (see page 16)

If a recipe calls for half a batch of this frosting, halve the quantities listed for a full recipe, but use 3 full eggs.

1. Melt the dark chocolate, unsweetened chocolate, and butter together in the top of a double boiler, stirring to keep the chocolate from burning, or microwave them together for 30 seconds at a time, stirring after each interval. Whisk the butter and chocolate briskly until they have combined; set aside.

2. Break the eggs into a medium saucepan and whisk them to break them up. Add the sugar, water, and salt and cook over medium-high heat, stirring continuously with a whisk and applying slight pressure to the sides and bottom of the pan so the mixture doesn't stick and overcook. Attach a candy thermometer to the side of the saucepan and cook, stirring with the whisk, until the mixture has reached 160°F.

3. Strain the egg mixture through a fine-mesh sieve into a bowl to remove any bits of overcooked egg, then whisk it into the chocolate mixture. Use an immersion blender to blend the frosting until completely smooth; alternatively, let the mixture cool, then blend it in a countertop blender, stopping to scrape the sides of the blender frequently. Let the frosting cool a bit, then refrigerate it until cool and fairly stiff. ★

Make Ahead
The frosting will keep in the refrigerator for up to 5 days. When ready to use, let it sit out for a bit or microwave it in 10-second intervals, stirring between each interval, until it is still stiff but soft enough to spread.

Chocolate Chip Almond Cake

Makes one 8-inch cake

This cake is one of our customers' favorites, but when we started making this moist, torte-like combination of rich brown butter and ground almonds studded with chunks of dark chocolate, we never intended to offer it on the menu. This dessert was created to be cut into tiny, bite-size squares and served as an amuse-bouche while our customers took their time looking at the menu. Almost immediately, however, we ran into a problem: guests would take a bite of the almond cake and say, "Oh, I'll have a slice of this." This happened night after night, until eventually servers gave in to appease our regular customers and created "slices" of the cake by lining up a dozen of the little pieces on a plate and covering them with chocolate sauce. That's when we knew that things would have to change. We started baking the batter in 8-inch round cake tins, developed a rich chocolate glaze to top it, and offered slices with a drizzle of caramel sauce and a scoop of vanilla ice cream. It's been a best-seller ever since. Pictured on page 15.

Cake

2 cups butter (4 sticks), at room temperature, plus extra for greasing the cake pan

9 large extra-large egg whites

1½ teaspoons pure vanilla extract

1½ teaspoons amaretto

2¾ cups confectioners' sugar

1 cup plus 2 tablespoons natural almond flour or ground almonds

¾ cup plus 2 tablespoons all-purpose flour

¼ teaspoon salt

3½ ounces dark chocolate (preferably 55% cacao), chopped into pieces roughly the size of chocolate chips

Chocolate Glaze

16 ounces dark chocolate (preferably 60% cacao), coarsely chopped

1½ cups (3 sticks) unsalted butter

¼ cup light corn syrup

2 tablespoons water

....

 tip

When sifting ingredients, like the confectioner's sugar, you can use a rubber spatula or a flexible pastry scraper to press them through the sieve.

....

Make the Cake

1. In a heavy-bottomed pot, melt the butter over medium to medium-high heat and continue to cook it, making sure not to let the foam bubble over. To check the color, scoop a little bit of the liquid out with a ladle. When the milk solids in the butter cook to a deep brown, the browned bits fall to the bottom of the pot, the liquid fat begins to take on a golden color, and the whole things smells nutty, remove from the heat and set aside to cool. The brown butter will continue to cook and darken as it cools.

2. Preheat the oven to 350°F. Cut a circle of parchment paper to fit the bottom of an 8-inch round cake pan. Butter the pan, line it with the parchment circle, and butter the parchment.

3. Warm the brown butter in the microwave or by putting the container in a bowl of hot water until the butter is fluid but not very warm. Measure out 1½ cups (set aside any extra brown butter for another use). In a small bowl, whisk together the egg whites, vanilla, and amaretto. Sift the sugar into a large bowl. Sift together the almond flour, flour, and salt and add them to bowl with the sugar. (If the almond skins don't fit through the sieve, fold them back into the sifted mixture.)

4. Whisk together the egg mixture and the dry ingredients until just combined. Using a rubber spatula, fold in the brown butter until fully combined, then fold in the chopped chocolate.

5. Pour the batter into the prepared pan and smooth the top with a small offset spatula or a rubber spatula. Bake for 1 hour and 15 minutes, until a paring knife inserted into the center of the cake comes out clean.

6. Let the cake cool to room temperature, then turn it upside down (shake the pan a bit if the cake won't slide out), and set it on a cooling rack. Remove the parchment paper. If you're not using the cake right away, wrap it in a double layer of plastic wrap and refrigerate or freeze it.

tip

If you're buttering a lot of cake pans, you can keep a small plastic container of softened butter on the counter and use a medium-size paintbrush to apply the butter to the pans.

Make the Glaze

Melt the chocolate and the butter together in the top of a double boiler, stirring to keep the chocolate from burning, or microwave them together in 30-seconds intervals, stirring after each interval, until they become liquid, about 1 minute and 30 seconds total. Using a whisk, mix the butter and chocolate briskly until combined. Whisk in the corn syrup and water until fully incorporated. Transfer the glaze to a quart-size container and store it in the refrigerator.

tip

To keep the cake from drying out after it has been cut, put pieces of parchment paper against the cut edges.

Assemble the Cake

1. Set the cake right-side up on a wire rack set over a sheet pan. With a bread knife, trim off the domed top of the cake and the raised edges, taking off just enough to make the cake flat. Brush off any crumbs, then invert the cake onto the wire rack so that the flat bottom of the cake becomes the top.

2. Warm the glaze in the microwave, stirring every 30 seconds, or by putting the container of glaze in a bowl of hot water and stirring until the glaze is fluid. Pour the glaze evenly over the top of the cake, making sure it runs down all the sides. Tap the entire pan firmly on the counter a few times so the excess glaze will slide off the cake.

3. Let the cake sit at room temperature until the glaze sets, about 20 minutes, or refrigerate for about 5 minutes. When the glaze is firm, run a long, thin knife or offset spatula under the cake to dislodge it from the wire rack and transfer it to a cake plate. ★

tip

If you want to decorate this cake, arrange chocolate pearls and cocoa nibs on top of the cake right after you pour on the glaze. The glaze will hold them in place once it cools.

Serving Suggestion

Caramel Sauce (page 162) and Vanilla Ice Cream (page 157)

Make Ahead

The brown butter can be made ahead and refrigerated for up to 3 weeks. Warm it in the microwave or by putting the container of butter into a bowl of hot water until the butter is fluid but not hot. The unglazed cake will keep in the refrigerator for up to 7 days or in the freezer for up to 1 month. The glaze will keep in the refrigerator for up to 2 weeks. If the cake and glaze aren't stored for very long before the cake is assembled, the whole thing can be refrigerated for 1 week.

Chocolate Hazelnut Mousse Cake

Makes one 8-inch cake

This rich, creamy cake of chocolate mousse layered with toasty hazelnuts and a rich, fudgy cake "crust" is made with what we like to call a truffle mousse—it's so dense and rich that you could almost make truffles with it. The mousse is made with a combination of milk chocolate, which gives it a lovely sweet flavor, and 100% dark chocolate, which keeps the texture of the mousse very smooth. It also contains both egg whites and a bit of gelatin, so the cake stays nice and firm when you slice it. We've made this cake with all kinds of nuts over the years—almonds, macadamias, peanuts, and cashews—but this is our favorite combination. (As with all our recipes that use uncooked egg, we use pasteurized eggs in the shop.)

Fudge Cake "Crust"

Vegetable oil spray

6 tablespoons all-purpose flour

2 tablespoons unsweetened Dutch-process cocoa powder

¼ teaspoon baking soda

Pinch of salt

3 tablespoons unsalted butter, at room temperature

¼ cup dark brown sugar

2 tablespoons granulated sugar

1 extra-large egg

2 tablespoons sour cream

¼ cup buttermilk or heavy cream

Hazelnut Butter Crunch

1¼ cups blanched, peeled hazelnuts

4½ teaspoons granulated sugar

1½ teaspoons vegetable oil

1½ ounces milk chocolate, in pastilles or coarsely chopped

1 tablespoon unsalted butter

¾ cup feuilletine (see page 132)

Truffle Mousse

11½ ounces milk chocolate, coarsely chopped

1¾ ounces unsweetened chocolate (preferably 100% cacao), coarsely chopped

2 teaspoons powdered gelatin

1½ cups heavy cream

4 extra-large egg yolks

1 teaspoon plus ¼ cup granulated sugar

3 tablespoons water

Special Tool

8-inch springform pan (see page 17)

....

If you can only find hazelnuts with skins, toast them as directed, then transfer them to a kitchen towel and rub them together in the towel while still warm to remove the skins. You can use any kind of nuts you like for this cake; if you use macadamia nuts, add almost no oil when making the nut butter because macadamia nuts contain a lot of oil on their own.

....

recipe continues on the next page

Make the Cake "Crust"

1. Preheat the oven to 350°F. Coat the sides and bottom of an 8-inch springform pan with vegetable oil spray.

2. In a small bowl, stir together the flour, cocoa powder, baking soda, and salt; set aside.

3. In the bowl of a stand mixer fitted with the paddle attachment, cream the butter and both sugars on medium speed for 1 minute. Stop the mixer and scrape down the sides and bottom of the bowl. Beat for 1 minute on medium, until the mixture is very light and fluffy. Add the egg and mix on medium-low for 20 seconds, stop the mixer to scrape the sides and bottom of the bowl, and mix again on medium until there are no lumps or unmixed ingredients, about 30 seconds.

4. Add the flour mixture to the batter and mix on low until just combined. Stop the mixer and scrape down the sides and bottom of the bowl. Add the sour cream and mix on low until just combined, then stop the mixer and scrape down the sides and bottom of the bowl again.

5. With the mixer on low, add the buttermilk in a thin stream, then mix on low until the batter is uniform, about 20 seconds. Remove the bowl and finish mixing by hand, using a rubber spatula in a beating motion and scraping the sides and bottom of the bowl to ensure that all the ingredients are evenly incorporated and the batter is completely smooth and lump-free.

6. Pour the batter into the prepared pan and use a rubber spatula to push it into a smooth, even layer (it will be very thin). Bake the cake for 10 to 15 minutes, until a paring knife inserted into the center comes out clean. Let the cake cool in the pan to room temperature. If the cake shrinks a bit while cooling, press it down firmly to spread it out with your fingers so that it fills the bottom of the pan.

Make the Crunch

1. Preheat the oven to 350°F, spread the hazelnuts in a single layer on a sheet pan and bake for 15 minutes.

2. Finely chop ⅓ cup of the toasted hazelnuts and set them aside. Put the remaining hazelnuts in a food processor with the sugar and grind them together. As the food processor is running, slowly pour in the vegetable oil, then let the processor run until the nuts release their oils and become a fairly smooth, runny paste, 3 to 4 minutes. If necessary, stop and scrape down the sides and bottom of the food processor bowl a few times to make sure all the nuts are processed.

 tip

When grinding the nut butter, it's best to use the nuts when they're still very hot so that they'll release their oils more quickly; even if the nuts are cool, however, they will eventually release enough oil to make a very runny nut paste.

3. Melt the chocolate and butter together in the top of a double boiler, stirring to keep the chocolate from burning, or microwave them together in 10- to 20-second intervals, stirring after each interval, until they become liquid. Whisk the butter and chocolate briskly until combined. Add the hazelnut butter to the melted chocolate and stir until well combined, then add the chopped hazelnuts and the feuilletine to the mixture and use a rubber spatula to fold everything together. Pour the mixture over the cake layer in the springform pan and use the back of a spoon to spread the mixture into a smooth layer. Put the entire pan in the freezer to set the crunch layer.

Make the Mousse and Assemble the Cake

1. Put both kinds of chocolate in a medium heatproof bowl and set it aside. Put the gelatin in a small bowl, mix it with 1 tablespoon of the cream, and set aside. In a small saucepan, heat the remaining cream over medium-high heat until it begins to steam. Remove the cream from the heat, pour about 3 tablespoons of the cream into the bowl with the gelatin and stir it a bit, then pour the remaining cream over the chocolate. Let both mixtures sit until the gelatin has softened and the hot liquid has melted the chocolate, about 3 minutes, then whisk the cream and chocolate briskly until they have combined. Add the gelatin mixture and whisk everything together.

2. In the bowl of a stand mixer fitted with the whisk attachment, whip the egg yolks and 1 teaspoon of the sugar for about 2 minutes, until the yolks are pale and form ribbons when the whisk is lifted out.

3. In a small pot, bring the water and the remaining ¼ cup sugar to a boil over high heat and let it boil for exactly 1 minute. With the mixer on low speed, pour the sugar syrup into the eggs in a slow, steady stream, then turn the mixer to high and whip until the side of the mixing bowl has cooled to room temperature, about 3 minutes; the mixture will be thick and sticky-looking. Scrape down the sides of the bowl and whip the mixture again for 30 seconds to make sure everything has been incorporated.

4. Remove the bowl from the mixer, add the chocolate-cream mixture, and use a rubber spatula to fold and mix everything together until there are no streaks in the mousse. Pour the mousse into the springform pan on top of the crunch layer and tap the pan firmly on the counter a few times to release any air bubbles trapped in the mousse. Smooth the top of the mousse with a rubber spatula or small offset spatula. (This cake is not covered with glaze, so you'll want to top to look as nice as possible.) Wrap the cake pan in plastic wrap and freeze for at least 6 hours, preferably overnight.

5. Remove the cake from the freezer and soak a kitchen towel in very hot water, wring it out, and wrap it around the sides of the pan. Run a paring knife between the top edge of the cake and the pan, then gently remove the sides of the pan. Heat a small offset spatula or a butter knife in very hot water, dry it, and use it to smooth out any raised edges or rough patches along the top, sides, and corners of the cake. Put the cake in the refrigerator until it is no longer frozen, at least 2 hours. ★

Make Ahead
The cake can be refrigerated for 3 to 4 days.

Single-Origin Flourless Chocolate Cake

Makes one 8-inch cake

A few years ago we tried making this cake using a single-origin chocolate. The result was so delicious and the flavors of the chocolate came through so well that we decided that the flourless cake on our regular menu should use a single-origin chocolate. We've tried making this cake with a variety of single-origin chocolates, but we were surprised to find that the chocolates reacted differently in the oven and the cakes' textures varied considerably. Now we always make this cake with a 70% cacao chocolate from Ecuador made by Arriba Gold. When making this cake at home, you may find that your favorite chocolate also changes the cake's texture, but even if the cake is a little softer or firmer than the one we serve in the cafés, the flavor of the chocolate you choose will come through wonderfully.

6½ ounces single-origin dark chocolate (preferably 70% cacao), coarsely chopped

9 tablespoons (1⅛ sticks) unsalted butter, plus extra for buttering the pan

¼ cup water

½ cup plus 2 tablespoons granulated sugar

3 extra-large eggs

Special Tool
8-inch springform pan (see page 17)

tip

If you don't have a baking pan wide enough to accommodate the cake pan, a 12-inch cake pan can make an excellent water bath.

1. Preheat the oven to 350°F. Cut a circle of parchment paper to fit the bottom of an 8-inch springform pan. Line the pan with the parchment circle, then butter the parchment. Wrap the sides and bottom of the pan in two layers of aluminum foil so that it is watertight.

2. Put the chocolate in a medium bowl and set it aside. In a medium saucepan, heat the butter, water, and ½ cup of the sugar until the butter melts and the sugar has dissolved; the mixture may start to bubble a little. Pour the hot liquid over the chocolate and let it sit until the chocolate has melted, about 1 minute, then whisk the ingredients together until the mixture is smooth; set it aside.

3. In the bowl of a stand mixer fitted with the whisk attachment, whip the eggs and the remaining 2 tablespoons sugar on medium-high for 2 minutes, until the eggs are light and frothy. Remove the bowl from the mixer, add the melted chocolate mixture, and use a rubber spatula to gently fold everything together until there are no visible streaks.

4. Pour the batter into the prepared pan. Place the cake pan into a baking pan at least 2 inches taller than the springform pan. Fill the outer pan with about ¾ inch water, then cover the whole thing tightly with aluminum foil. (Make sure the foil is pulled tight so it doesn't sag over the cake.) Use a paring knife to poke three holes in each corner of the aluminum foil to let steam out.

5. Transfer the pans to the oven and bake for 50 to 60 minutes. When ready, the cake should be set and may have little craters where air bubbles have popped and firmed up, but it might still look wet in the very center and jiggle when the pan is moved. (You can touch the top of the cake very gently with your finger to make sure that it is set; some may come off on your fingers, but it will be thick, not liquid.) Remove the whole pan from the oven, set it aside to cool to room temperature, then take the cake out of the water bath and unwrap the foil from the bottom of the springform pan. Wrap the cake in plastic wrap and refrigerate it for at least 4 hours, preferably overnight.

6. Remove the cake from the refrigerator and unwrap it. Soak a kitchen towel in very hot water, wring it out, and wrap it around the sides of the pan. Gently remove the sides of the pan, then flip the cake onto a serving plate. Reheat the towel, wring it out, and lay it over the bottom of the pan that is still adhered to the cake, until the towel is no longer warm. Gently remove the bottom of the pan from the cake, then remove the parchment paper and serve. ★

Make Ahead
This cake can be kept in the refrigerator for 1 week.

Serving Suggestion
Raspberry Chambord Sauce (page 162) and Vanilla Whipped Cream (page 160)

In the cafés, we use a kitchen torch instead of a hot towel to coax the cake out of the pan. This allows us to bake the cake without parchment paper, so that it has a smoother top. Run the torch lightly over the outer ring of the pan (just to soften the butter the pan was prepared with) and remove it. Invert the cake onto the serving plate, lightly torch the flat bottom of the pan, and gently slide it off the cake. If it doesn't slide easily, heat the bottom a little more.

German Chocolate Cake

Makes one 9-inch three-layer cake

Despite its name, German chocolate cake is a purely American invention. This delicious chocolate cake layered with rich coconut-and-pecan-filled custard was invented in the 1950s in Texas, and it owes its name to the fact that it was made with Baker's German's Sweet Chocolate (a popular baking chocolate developed by a man named Sam German). Our version is a little different from most—in addition to filling and topping the cake with the usual coconut-and-nut custard, we also cover the sides of the cake with our creamy chocolate frosting to keep the whole thing moist.

1 cup unsweetened shredded coconut

1 cup sweetened shredded coconut

1½ cups pecans, finely chopped

12 ounces evaporated milk

1¾ cups granulated sugar

3 extra-large egg yolks

1 teaspoon pure vanilla extract

½ cup (1 stick) unsalted butter

¾ cup water

3 (9-inch) layers Chocolate Layer Cake (page 27), wrapped and refrigerated or frozen

½ recipe Chocolate Frosting (page 31)

8 pecan halves

recipe continues on the next page

1. In a large bowl, mix both kinds of coconut with the chopped pecans. Set a fine-mesh sieve over the bowl and set aside.

2. Combine the evaporated milk, 1 cup of the sugar, the egg yolks, and the vanilla in a large saucepan and whisk to combine. Add the butter and cook over high heat, whisking occasionally, until the butter has melted and the mixture comes to a boil. Boil for 3 minutes, whisking continuously. The mixture will thicken a little bit and will have thick, goopy bubbles. Pour the custard through the sieve onto the coconut mixture. Mix the custard with the coconut and pecans with a wooden spoon, making sure there are no clumps of dry coconut. Set the coconut custard aside to cool to room temperature.

3. Combine the remaining ¾ cup sugar and the water in a small saucepan and heat over medium heat, stirring occasionally, until the sugar has dissolved; set the simple syrup aside.

4. Remove the three cake layers from the refrigerator or freezer. If they're frozen, let them sit for 5 to 10 minutes. With a bread knife, cut the dome and any raised edges off each cake layer, taking off as much as necessary to create a flat, even surface.

5. Set one layer on a cake stand or flat plate. With a pastry brush, coat the top of the cake with one-third of the simple syrup. Top the cake layer with 1 to 1¼ cups of the coconut custard and use a small offset spatula or butter knife to spread it in an even layer almost to the edge of the cake. Take a second cake layer, turn it upside down, and set it on top of the custard. Brush more simple syrup onto this layer and top it with another 1 to 1¼ cups of the custard. Top the custard with the last cake layer, placing it upside down. Brush with the remaining simple syrup. Spread another 1 to 1¼ cups of the custard on top of the cake.

6. Apply the chocolate frosting evenly over the sides of the cake. (See page 24 for our favorite frosting technique.) The frosting should come all the way up the sides of the cake and cover the edges of the top layer of coconut custard. (If you have extra frosting, you can put decorative "beading" on the bottom of the cake; see "Using a Pastry Bag," page 108.) Decorate the top of the cake with the pecan halves, and refrigerate the entire cake for at least 2 hours to let it firm up. ★

....

 tip

Don't put too much coconut custard between the cake layers or the pieces of coconut and pecan will make the cake difficult to slice.

....

Make Ahead
The coconut filling can be refrigerated for up to 3 days. Reheat it in the microwave in 10-second intervals, stirring after each interval, until it comes up to room temperature and will spread without tearing up the layers of cake. The assembled cake will keep in the refrigerator for 2 to 3 days.

Above and Beyond
German Chocolate Ice Cream Parfait
If you have any leftover coconut-pecan custard, layer it with chocolate ice cream and top the whole thing with whipped cream. ★

Checkerboard Cake

Makes one 6-inch cake

The checkerboard cake is a wonderful illusion, a combination of vanilla and chocolate cake arranged in a bull's-eye pattern and stacked in alternating layers so that when you cut into it, each slice has a checkerboard pattern. The checkerboard cake first appeared in the early 1900s, and cooks have used a wide variety of techniques to get the pattern. There have been recipes that called for using coffee cans and biscuit cutters, recipes that used jelly-roll pans, and recipes that called for making rings out of aluminum foil to keep the batters separate. You can even buy a set of pans designed just to make checkerboard cakes.

Our version uses small cake pans and ring cutters to produce extra-small checkerboard squares so that you get some of the chocolate cake, the buttery vanilla cake, and our smooth, creamy chocolate buttercream frosting in every bite. It's one of the most delicious—and stunning—cakes we've ever eaten!

Vanilla Batter

2 extra-large eggs

1 teaspoon pure vanilla extract

1¼ cups cake flour

3½ teaspoons baking powder

¼ teaspoon salt

6 tablespoons (¾ stick) unsalted butter, at room temperature, plus extra for greasing the cake pans

1¼ cups granulated sugar

½ cup sour cream

½ cup whole milk

Chocolate Batter

2 extra-large eggs

½ teaspoon pure vanilla extract

1 cup cake flour

1 teaspoon baking soda

¼ teaspoon salt

6 tablespoons (¾ stick) unsalted butter, at room temperature, plus extra for greasing the cake pans

1 cup dark brown sugar

⅓ cup unsweetened Dutch-processed cocoa powder, sifted

⅓ cup sour cream

½ cup cold coffee or milk

Chocolate Buttercream Frosting

1½ cups (3 sticks) unsalted butter, at room temperature

7½ ounces dark chocolate (preferably 70% cacao), coarsely chopped

1½ ounces white chocolate

2 extra-large eggs

1 extra-large egg white

½ teaspoon pure vanilla extract

¼ teaspoon salt

¾ cup granulated sugar

3 tablespoons water

1½ teaspoons light corn syrup

Simple Syrup

¼ cup granulated sugar

¼ cup water

Special Tools

6-inch cake pans (see page 17)

3¾-inch, 2-inch, and 1-inch ring cutters (see page 21)

recipe continues on the next page

Make the Vanilla Cake Layers

1. Preheat the oven to 350°F. Cut circles of parchment paper to fit the bottoms of two 6-inch round cake pans. Butter the pans, line them with the parchment circles, and butter the parchment.

2. In a small bowl, beat the eggs lightly with the vanilla until they are broken up. In a large bowl, sift together the cake flour, baking powder, and salt. Set both bowls aside.

3. In the bowl of a stand mixer fitted with the paddle attachment, cream the butter and granulated sugar on medium speed for 3 minutes, until the mixture is very light and fluffy. Add the egg mixture and continue mixing on medium-low until the mixture just comes together, about 20 seconds. Stop the mixer and scrape down the sides and bottom of the bowl very well to incorporate any unmixed ingredients, then mix on medium for another 15 seconds, until there are no lumps or unmixed ingredients.

4. Add one-third of the sifted flour mixture and mix on low until just combined. Stop the mixer, scrape down the sides and bottom of the bowl, and add half the sour cream. Mix on low until just incorporated, about 30 seconds, then stop the mixer and scrape down the sides and bottom. Repeat with another third of the dry ingredients and the remaining sour cream, scraping the bowl well after each addition. Add the remaining flour mixture, mix until just incorporated, and scrape the bowl again.

5. With the mixer on low, pour the milk into the batter in a thin stream, then mix on low until the batter is uniform, about 20 seconds.

6. Remove the bowl from the mixer and finish mixing by hand, using a rubber spatula in a beating motion and scraping the sides and bottom of the bowl to ensure that all the ingredients are evenly incorporated and the batter is completely smooth and lump-free.

7. Divide the batter between the prepared pans and bake for 25 to 35 minutes, until a paring knife inserted into the center of the cakes comes out clean. Let the cakes cool to room temperature, then remove them from the pans, remove the parchment paper, wrap each layer in two layers of plastic wrap, and put them in the refrigerator or freezer to chill.

Make the Chocolate Cake Layers

Follow all the instructions for the vanilla cake layers, but use 1 teaspoon of baking soda for the baking powder, brown sugar for granulated, and add the cocoa powder to the butter mixture just after the eggs. Beat the batter on low until the cocoa is just incorporated. Substitute the coffee for the milk. Bake for 30 to 40 minutes.

Make the Frosting

1. Cut the butter into slices ¼ to ½ inch thick and set them aside.

2. Melt the dark chocolate in the top of a double boiler, stirring to keep it from burning, or microwave it in 15-second intervals, stirring after each interval, until it becomes liquid. Melt the white chocolate in the top of a double boiler, stirring to keep it burning, or microwave it in 10-second intervals, stirring after each interval, until it becomes liquid. Cover both bowls of melted chocolate to keep warm and set them aside.

3. In the bowl of a stand mixer fitted with the whisk attachment, whip the eggs, egg white, vanilla, and salt on medium speed until the eggs are frothy, about 2 minutes, then turn the mixer to low.

4. In a small saucepan, combine the granulated sugar, water, and corn syrup. Bring the mixture to a boil over high heat, stirring occasionally. When the mixture starts to boil, let it boil for exactly 1 minute. With the mixer running on medium, slowly pour the syrup into the egg mixture in a thin, steady stream about the width of pencil, making sure not to pour it onto the sides of the bowl, where it will stick and solidify. Turn the mixer to high and whip until the side of the mixing bowl has cooled to room temperature, about 3 minutes.

5. Turn the mixer to low and drop the pieces of butter into the mixer one at a time, waiting 10 seconds between each piece. As the butter is added, the mixture will begin to thicken and look curdled. When all the butter has been added, turn the mixer to high and whisk for 30 seconds.

6. Remove ½ cup of the mixture and set it aside to make into white chocolate buttercream.

7. Check the temperature of the melted dark chocolate, and if it's no longer fluid, reheat it a bit. Turn the mixer to low and slowly pour the dark chocolate into the butter mixture, then mix on medium until the frosting is smooth. (The heat of the chocolate will melt the butter just a little and will fix the frosting's curdled appearance.) Turn the mixer to high and whip for 1 minute to make the frosting fluffy.

8. Check the temperature of the melted white chocolate, and if it's no longer fluid, reheat it a bit. Pour it into the reserved butter mixture and whisk by hand until the frosting is smooth.

....

 tip

When making the buttercream, if the butter is not totally soft, you can squish each piece with your fingers before you add it so that it will incorporate into the frosting.

....

Assemble the Cake

1. Combine the sugar and water in a small saucepan and heat over medium heat, stirring occasionally, until the sugar has dissolved; set the simple syrup aside.

2. Remove the chocolate and vanilla cake layers from the freezer and let them sit for 5 to 10 minutes, but don't worry about thawing them—the cake will be easier to work with if it's still semi-frozen. With a bread knife, cut the dome and any raised edges off each layer of cake, taking off as much as necessary to create a flat, even surface. Set the cake tops aside; they will be turned into crumbs to coat the cake. Set all four layers next to one another and trim the tops so that they are all the same height.

3. Cut each cake layer in half horizontally so that you have eight layers. (For the easiest way to get even layers, see "How to Assemble and Frost a Perfect, Showstopping Cake," page 24.) Remove one of the thin chocolate layers and one of the thin vanilla layers and set them aside with the cake tops. You should have three chocolate and three vanilla layers left to work with.

4. Using 3¾-, 2-, and 1-inch ring cutters, cut the cake layers so that each layer becomes three rings and one center circle. (Use a ruler to center the cutters so that the rings are as even as possible.) Once all the layers have been cut, gently rearrange them so that they form bull's-eye patterns: Three of the layers will start with a chocolate outer ring, followed by a vanilla ring just inside it, a chocolate ring inside that, and a vanilla circle in the center; three of the layers will have a vanilla outer ring, a chocolate ring just inside it, a vanilla ring inside that, and a chocolate circle in the middle.

5. Put a dab of chocolate buttercream on your cake plate, and place one of the bull's-eye cake layers on the plate. With a pastry brush, coat the top of the cake with some of the simple syrup and let the cake sit for a minute so the syrup will soak in. Spread a thin layer of chocolate buttercream over the layer of cake. Take a second bull's-eye layer of cake and set it on the first layer, pressing it down gently so that the buttercream holds the layers together (if your first layer had a ring of chocolate cake on the outside, this second layer should have a ring of vanilla cake on the outside). Brush the new layer with simple syrup and top with buttercream. Repeat this process with the remaining layers of cake alternating between layers with chocolate on the outside and layers with vanilla on the outside. Wrap the cake in plastic wrap and refrigerate it for 30 minutes to help it firm up.

recipe continues on the next page

tip

If the rings of cake break as you're rearranging them, gently push them back into place; the checkerboard pieces are so small that once the cake is sliced, the breaks won't affect the result.

6. Break the extra cake layers and the cut-off tops into chunks about 2 inches wide, spread them on a sheet pan, and bake them at 250°F for 20 minutes to dry them out a bit. Let the scraps cool, then transfer them to a food processor and pulse them into fine crumbs. Sift the crumbs through a sieve and discard or re-grind the larger pieces.

7. When the cake has chilled, remove it from the refrigerator. Spread a thin layer of dark chocolate buttercream on the sides of the cake; the sides should be covered, but some cake can show through.

8. Put the remaining dark chocolate buttercream and the white chocolate buttercream into two pastry bags fitted with ½-inch circular tips. Pipe stripes of buttercream onto the top of the cake, alternating between the dark chocolate and white chocolate; the stripes should touch one another and should cover the entire top of the cake. Turn the cake so that the stripes are aligned up and down (rather than side to side). With the tip of a paring knife, make a line through the stripes, going left to right; dragging the knife through the stripes will cause a bit of the dark chocolate to travel into the white and visa versa. Repeat the drag mark to make horizontal "stripes" going left to right all across the cake, keeping the drag marks ¼ inch apart, then make drag marks going left to right in between the first ones. The result will look like a nonpareil marbling pattern.

9. When the top of the cake is done, use the palm of your hand to gently pat the crumbs onto the sides of the cake, making sure to fully cover the sides all the way to the top. (This will hide the edges of the frosting on the top of the cake too.) Chill the cake before serving to help the frosting firm up. ★

Make Ahead
The cake layers can be refrigerated for up to 5 days or frozen for up 1 month. The buttercream can be refrigerated for up to 5 days. Bring it up to room temperature or microwave it for 10 seconds and then stir it well; repeat until it is soft enough to work with.

To make a really bold pattern on the top of the cake, you can use some of our regular Chocolate Frosting (page 31) alongside the white chocolate buttercream instead of using the dark chocolate buttercream.

This cake is easiest to serve if it is cut into nice thick wedges so that the individual pieces of the checkerboard pattern will stay in place when the slices are transferred to plates.

Above and Beyond
Vanilla Cupcakes
One batch of vanilla cake batter will make about 18 cupcakes. Preheat the oven to 350°F. Line muffin tins with paper liners. Fill each cup with about ¼ cup batter (we use an ice cream scoop to portion the batter so that the cupcakes are even—and because it's the least messy way to fill the cups). Bake for 20 minutes. Frost with the Chocolate Frosting (page 31) using a pastry bag fitted with a star tip or a knife or small offset spatula. ★

Turtle Cheesecake

Makes one 9-inch cake

This is a classic New York–style cheesecake with a twist. It's dense and creamy but just light enough that each bite is substantial without being heavy. The bottom "crust" is actually a thin layer of our rich chocolate layer cake. And the "turtle" part of the cake comes from our Chocolate Syrup and Caramel Syrup, which we swirl onto the cake and then top with pecans, all before the cake even goes into the oven. When the cake is done, it is finished with even more chocolate, caramel, and pecans for extra flavor and crunch.

1 (9-inch) layer of chocolate cake (see page 29), chilled in the refrigerator

2 cups granulated sugar

¼ cup all-purpose flour

½ cup sour cream

¼ cup heavy cream

1 teaspoon pure vanilla extract

4½ (8-ounce) packages cream cheese, at room temperature

6 extra-large eggs, at room temperature

Vegetable oil spray

½ cup Chocolate Syrup (page 162)

½ cup Caramel Sauce (page 162)

1 cup pecan halves, coarsely chopped

Special Tools

9-inch springform pan (the sides should be at least 2½ inches tall) (see page 17)

Squeeze bottles for the chocolate and caramel syrups (optional, see page 20)

1. Preheat the oven to 325°F. With a bread knife, cut the dome and any raised edges off the chocolate cake layer, taking off as much as necessary to create a flat, even surface. Cut the cake in half horizontally so that you have two layers. (For the easiest way to get even layers, see "How to Assemble and Frost a Perfect, Showstopping Cake," page 24.) Put the bottom layer of the chocolate cake into the springform pan; if the cake shrank a bit while cooling, press it down firmly with your fingers to spread it out so that it fills the bottom of the pan. (Discard the remaining half of the cake or use it to make a cake shake, see page 48.)

2. In a small bowl, mix together the sugar and the flour. In a separate bowl, mix together the sour cream, heavy cream, and vanilla. Set both bowls aside.

3. In the bowl of a stand mixer fitted with the paddle attachment, beat the cream cheese on medium-high for 3 minutes, until it is very creamy and smooth. Stop the mixer and use a rubber spatula to scrape down the sides and bottom of the bowl. With the mixer on low, slowly pour in the sugar-flour mixture; continue mixing until the dry ingredients are just incorporated, then stop the mixer and scrape down the sides and bottom of the bowl. Add the sour cream mixture and mix on low until just incorporated, then stop the mixer and scrape down the sides and bottom of the bowl again.

recipe continues on the next page

4. With the mixer on low, add the eggs one at a time, waiting until each is incorporated before adding the next. Remove the bowl from the mixer and finish mixing by hand, using a rubber spatula in a beating motion and scraping down the sides and bottom of the bowl to ensure that the batter is very smooth.

5. Wrap the sides and bottom of a 9-inch springform pan in two layers of aluminum foil so that it is watertight, and spray the inside of the pan with vegetable oil spray. Pour the batter into the springform pan, on top of the layer of chocolate cake. Use a squeeze bottle, spoon, or pastry bag to drizzle a scant ¼ cup of the chocolate syrup onto the batter in a curlicue pattern. Insert a small offset spatula or butter knife 1 to 1½ inches into the top of the cake and swirl it all around in small circles. Repeat with a scant ¼ cup of the caramel sauce. Sprinkle ⅓ cup of the chopped pecans on top of the cake, and stir them in just a little bit so that they sink into the batter a bit but are still visible.

6. Put the filled springform pan into a baking pan at least 2 inches taller than the springform pan. Fill the outer pan with about ¾ inch of water. Bake the cake for 3 hours. The cake will rise about 1 inch as it bakes, but it will settle down a bit as it cools.

7. Remove the whole pan from the oven, then take the cake out of the water bath and unwrap the foil. Let the cake cool to room temperature, then wrap it loosely in plastic wrap and refrigerate for at least 6 hours, preferably overnight.

8. When the cake has chilled, remove the pan from the fridge and unwrap it. Heat the sides of the pan very quickly with a kitchen torch or soak a kitchen towel in very hot water, wring it out, and wrap it around the sides of the pan. Gently remove the sides of the pan. Sprinkle the remaining ⅔ cup pecans on the cake and drizzle the remaining ¼ cup chocolate sauce and caramel sauce on top of the cake in a zigzag pattern, allowing them to drip down the sides of the cake a little. Chill the cake until you're ready to serve it. To cut the cake, heat a chef's knife by running it under very hot water and then wipe it dry. Repeat for every slice of cake to keep the knife hot. ★

Make Ahead

The cake can be kept in the refrigerator for 3 to 4 days before topping it with the pecans and chocolate and caramel sauces.

When stirring in the chocolate and caramel sauces, don't put the knife or spatula too far into the cake or you'll pull up some of the chocolate cake "crust" and end up with crumbs in the cheesecake.

Above and Beyond
Chocolate Cake Shake

Instead of throwing out the scraps from the chocolate cake crust, use them to make an ice cream shake, a dessert dreamed up by our pastry assistant Jeremy Molina: Combine 2 big scoops of Vanilla Ice Cream (page 157) with ½ cup of the chocolate cake, a scant ¼ cup whipped cream, and ¾ cup whole milk in a blender and process until smooth. Serve topped with more whipped cream. ★

Peanut Butter Cheesecake
recipe on page 50

Turtle Cheesecake
recipe on page 47

Peanut Butter Cheesecake

Makes one 9-inch cake

This delicious peanut butter and chocolate cheesecake is almost more of a custard than a cake; it bakes very slowly in a water bath until it is firm enough to cut slices out of but still smooth, creamy, and very tender. Once it cools, the cheesecake is covered with our rich chocolate glaze, which is made from dark chocolate with 55% cacao and has just enough bitterness to balance the sweetness and saltiness of the peanut butter perfectly. The result is like a huge, grown-up version of a peanut butter cup, to be eaten in thick slices. Pictured on page 49.

Cookie Crumb Crust

3 tablespoons unsalted butter

2 cups Chocolate Cookie Crumbs (page 78)

2 teaspoons granulated sugar

¼ teaspoon salt

Cheesecake

1½ cups natural peanut butter with salt

4½ (8-ounce) packages cream cheese, at room temperature

½ cup dark brown sugar

1 cup granulated sugar

7 extra-large eggs

½ cup sour cream

2 teaspoons pure vanilla extract

Pinch of salt

Vegetable oil spray

To Assemble

Chocolate Glaze (page 60)

1½ cups peanuts, coarsely chopped

Special Tool

9-inch springform pan (the sides should be at least 2½ inches tall) (see page 17)

 tip

If you don't have a baking pan deep enough for the water bath, you can make one by using your deepest pan and wrapping it in a couple layers of heavy-duty aluminum foil to give it taller sides.

Make the Crust

Preheat the oven to 350°F. Melt the butter and mix it with the cookie crumbs, granulated sugar, and salt in a small bowl. Using your fingers, press the crumb mixture into the bottom of a 9-inch springform pan with 2½-inch-tall sides, filling the pan all the way to the edges and keeping it as even as possible. Bake the crust for 15 minutes. Remove from the oven, and let cool to room temperature.

Make the Cheesecake

1. Preheat the oven to 350°F. In the bowl of a stand mixer fitted with the paddle attachment, cream the peanut butter and cream cheese together on medium-low until they're just combined, about 30 seconds. Use a rubber spatula to scrape down the sides and bottom of the bowl and then mix for a few seconds until well combined.

2. With the mixer on low, slowly pour in the brown sugar and then the granulated sugar, and mix until they are just incorporated. Add the eggs one at a time, waiting until each is incorporated before adding the next and stopping the mixer after every 2 or 3 eggs to scrape down the sides and bottom of the bowl.

3. In a small bowl, mix the sour cream, vanilla, and salt. Add this mixture to the batter and mix on low until just incorporated. Remove the bowl from the mixer and finish mixing by hand, using a rubber spatula in a beating motion and scraping down the sides and bottom of the bowl to ensure that all the ingredients are evenly incorporated and the batter is very smooth.

4. Wrap the sides and bottom of the springform pan in two layers of aluminum foil so that it is watertight, and spray the inside of the pan with vegetable oil spray. Pour the batter into the pan and tap the whole thing firmly on the counter so that any air bubbles will rise to the surface. Smooth the top of the batter with a small offset or rubber spatula.

5. Put the filled pan into a baking pan at least 2 inches taller than the springform pan. Fill the outer pan with about ¾ inch of water, then cover the whole thing with aluminum foil. (Make sure the foil is pulled tightly and doesn't sag over the cake.) Use a paring knife to poke three holes in each corner of the aluminum foil to let steam out.

6. Bake the cheesecake for 2 hours, until it is firmly set. Remove the whole pan from the oven, let it cool to room temperature, then take the cake out of the water bath and unwrap the foil. Wrap the cake in plastic wrap and refrigerate it for at least 6 hours, preferably overnight.

7. When the cake has chilled, remove it from the fridge and unwrap it. Heat the sides of the pan very quickly with a kitchen torch or soak a kitchen towel in very hot water, wring it out, and wrap it around the sides of the pan. Gently remove the sides of the pan and return the cake to the refrigerator to chill for at least 30 minutes.

Assemble the Cake

1. Set the cake on a wire rack over a sheet pan. Pour the glaze onto the cake slowly, first covering as much of the sides as possible and then covering the top. Use a large offset spatula to gently smooth the top of the glaze, pushing the excess toward any spots on the sides of the cake that are not fully covered. When the cake is fully glazed, tap the entire pan firmly on the counter a few times to help excess glaze slide off the cake. Return the cake to the refrigerator to set for 5 minutes.

2. When the glaze has chilled, use your hands to gently press small handfuls of the chopped peanuts onto the sides of the cake so they stick to the glaze. Chill the cake in the refrigerator or freezer to firm up the glaze. To cut the cake, heat a chef's knife by running it under very hot water and then wipe it dry. Repeat for every slice of cake to keep the knife hot. ★

Make Ahead

The finished cake can be kept in the refrigerator for 3 to 4 days.

Chocolate Pineapple Upside-Down Cake

Yields one 10-inch cake

Pineapple upside-down cake, a staple of midcentury American cooking, was a special treat for Jon when he was growing up. He first fell in love with this cake when his neighbor Beverly Corris made it, and all through his childhood she would make it for him at Christmas every year. On Christmas Eve, Jon's parents would throw an enormous party for the whole neighborhood, and every year Mrs. Corris would bring over a cake and say, "Here you go, Jonny. Here's your pineapple cake." Our take on this classic cake is essentially just a chocolate version of the one that Mrs. Corris used to make. It starts with a batter that is very similar to our chocolate layer cake, but as the cake bakes, the caramel on the bottom of the pan and the juices from the fruit combine to create a rich, flavorful syrup that seeps into the cake and makes it rich and fudgy and flavorful.

Fruit and Caramel Base

1 medium-large pineapple, sweet-smelling but not overripe

Vegetable oil spray

¾ cup (1½ sticks) unsalted butter

1¼ cups dark brown sugar

Cake

1 bag of black tea (preferably a chocolate-flavored tea)

¾ cup boiling water

3 extra-large eggs

1 teaspoon vanilla extract

1¾ cups cake flour

¾ cup unsweetened Dutch-processed cocoa powder

1½ teaspoons baking soda

¼ teaspoon salt

9 tablespoons unsalted butter, softened

2¼ cups dark brown sugar

¾ cup plain yogurt

Special Tools

3- and 1-inch ring cutters (optional, see page 21)

Make the Base

1. Use a bread knife to cut the top off of the pineapple, making as flat a cut as possible. Without peeling the pineapple, cut it into ¼-inch-thick rings. (To get even slices, use the knife to mark the ¼ inch around all of the fruit, then slice through following those marks.) Use the larger of the two ring cutters to cut a 3-inch circle out of each slice of fruit, then use the small, 1-inch ring cutter to remove the fruit's fibrous core.

(Alternatively, you can cut rings of roughly this size and shape with a chef's knife.)

2. Cut a circle of parchment paper the same size as the bottom of a 10-inch cake pan. Coat the bottom and sides of the cake pan with vegetable oil spray, line the bottom of the pan with the cut parchment, and then spray the top of the parchment.

3. In a medium pot, heat the butter and brown sugar over high heat, whisking occasionally to keep the sugar from burning, until the butter has melted and the sugar has turned to liquid. Pour this caramel base into the prepared cake pan.

4. Arrange the pineapple rings in the cake pan, nestling them into the caramel base. (You should be able to fit 7 rings in a circle along the edge of the pan and 1 ring in the center.) Set the pan aside so the caramel base can cool and firm up.

Make the Cake

1. Steep the bag of tea in the boiling water and set it aside to brew for 10 minutes. When the tea is done, discard the tea bag and set the tea aside to cool to room temperature.

2. Preheat the oven to 350°F. In a small bowl, beat the eggs lightly with the vanilla until they are broken up. In a medium bowl, sift together the cake flour, cocoa powder, baking soda, and salt. Set both bowls aside.

3. In a stand mixer fitted with the paddle attachment, cream the butter and brown sugar on medium speed for 3 minutes, until the mixture is very light and fluffy. Add the egg mixture and continue mixing on medium-low until the mixture just comes together, about 30 seconds. Stop the mixer to scrape the bottom and sides of the bowl to incorporate any unmixed ingredients, then mix on medium for another 30 seconds until there are no lumps or unincorporated ingredients.

4. Add about one-third of the sifted flour mixture to the batter and mix on low until it is just combined. Stop the mixer, scrape down the sides and bottom of the bowl, and add about half of the yogurt to the batter. Mix on low until just incorporated, about 30 seconds, then stop the mixer and scrape the bowl. Repeat with another third of the dry ingredients and the remaining sour cream, scraping the bowl well after each addition. Add the remaining third of the flour mixture, mix until just incorporated, and scrape the bowl again.

5. Turn the mixer to low and add the tea, pouring it into the batter in a thin stream, then continue to mix on low until the batter is uniform, about 20 seconds.

6. Remove the bowl from the mixer and finish mixing by hand, using a rubber spatula in a beating motion and scraping the bottom and sides of bowl to ensure that all the ingredients are evenly incorporated and that the batter is completely smooth and lump-free.

7. Pour the batter into the pan, on top of the pineapple and caramel base, and tap the pan on the counter gently to remove any air bubbles and to help it settle around the rings of fruit. Bake for 50 minutes. (The top of the cake will probably have a crack or two in it, and the caramel from the bottom of the pan may seep up to the top and streak the sides of the cake a bit.)

8. When you remove the pan from the oven, let the cake sit for exactly 15 minutes, then run a paring knife or a small offset spatula along the edges of the cake to loosen it, place a large serving plate upside-down on top of the pan, and flip the cake onto the plate. Tap the bottom of the pan firmly a few times to loosen the fruit, then remove the pan. (If you unmold the cake too early, it may fall apart, or the caramel may slide off of the top; if you wait too long, the pineapple may become stuck to the bottom of the pan.) If some of the pineapple rings do not come out of the pan cleanly, you can use a small offset spatula to gently scoop them up and flip them into place; the cake is very moist and will hide little imperfections.

9. Put the cake in the refrigerator for at least 1 hour to let the caramel cool and solidify. ★

Make Ahead

The finished cake can be kept in the refrigerator for 3 to 4 days.

Chocolate Strawberry Shortcakes

Makes 12 shortcakes

There's something so very simple and so very wonderful about the combination of chocolate and strawberries. Every Valentine's Day we sell dozens of fresh strawberries dipped in chocolate, but our favorite way of combining these two flavors is in this chocolaty version of strawberry shortcakes. This dessert, made up of shortcakes flavored with a hefty helping of rich cocoa powder and topped with a generous drizzle of chocolate syrup, is a summer favorite. It captures the flavors of the season better than anything else we can think of.

¾ cup heavy cream

1¼ cups buttermilk, plus extra for brushing on the cakes

2 extra-large egg yolks

3 cups all-purpose flour, plus extra for dusting

½ cup unsweetened Dutch-process cocoa powder

⅔ cup plus ¼ cup granulated sugar

1½ tablespoons baking powder

2 teaspoons baking soda

½ teaspoon salt

1 cup (2 sticks) unsalted butter, cut into ¼- to ½-inch pieces and frozen

Raw or granulated sugar, for dusting

2 pints strawberries, hulled and quartered

Chocolate Syrup (page 162)

Vanilla Whipped Cream (page 160)

Special Tool

2¾-inch biscuit cutter (or a cup or empty can of a similar diameter)

 tip

If you can't fit sheet pans in your freezer, you can crowd the shortcakes onto a cutting board to freeze them, then transfer them to the sheet pans with a small offset spatula.

1. Preheat the oven to 375°F. Line two sheet pans with parchment paper or silicone liners. In a small bowl, whisk together the cream, buttermilk, and egg yolks; set aside. In a food processor, combine the flour, cocoa powder, ⅔ cup of the granulated sugar, the baking powder, baking soda, and salt and pulse a few times to mix them together. Add the frozen butter to the food processor and pulse until the largest pieces of butter are no bigger than peas.

2. Transfer the flour-butter mixture to a large bowl and make a wide well in the center. Pour the cream mixture into the well and mix everything together with a fork until all the ingredients are combined, then use your hands to gently fold the batter together until the last of the dry ingredients have been incorporated. (The dough will be very sticky.)

3. Generously flour the counter or a large sheet pan and turn the dough out onto the surface. Sprinkle flour on top of the dough and gently flatten it into a disk, then fold the dough and reflatten four to six times with your hands or a bench scraper, flouring the counter as necessary, until the dough is still sticky but is not sticking to the counter or your fingers in large chunks. Gently press out the dough until it is ¾ to 1 inch thick.

recipe continues on the next page

4. Put 1 inch of flour into a small bowl; dip the biscuit cutter into the flour and press it into the corner of the dough, then pull the cutter straight out without twisting it. (Twisting the cutter as you cut shortcakes will pinch their edges together and keep them from rising properly.) Place the shortcake on the prepared sheet pan, dip the cutter back into the flour, and repeat for the remaining shortcakes. When you've cut as many as you can, you can gently press the dough scraps together once (without kneading) and use them to cut more shortcakes, for a total of 12. Make sure there's at least 1½ inches between the shortcakes on the pan so they have room to spread. Brush each shortcake with buttermilk and sprinkle with a large pinch of raw sugar.

5. Place the sheet pan in the freezer for 10 minutes; this will help the shortcakes rise instead of spreading. Bake for 5 minutes, then reduce the oven temperature to 350°F and bake for another 10 minutes. Remove the shortcakes from the oven and let cool to room temperature.

6. In a medium bowl, toss the strawberries with the remaining ¼ cup granulated sugar and set them aside to macerate at room temperature until the sugar has dissolved and the berries have released some of their juices.

7. Cut the shortcakes in half horizontally and place the bottom halves on dessert plates. Place a large spoonful of the berries (¼ to ⅓ cup) on each of the bottom halves, drizzle chocolate syrup on top of the strawberries, and top them with a large dollop of whipped cream. Lean the top halves of the shortcakes against the strawberries and serve. ★

Make Ahead
The shortcakes can be kept in an airtight container at room temperature for 3 to 4 days.

Chocolate Cuatro Leches Cake

Makes one 9 x 13-inch cake

The *tres leches* or "three milks" cake is an incredibly popular dessert all across Latin America, including in Puerto Rico, where our executive pastry chef, Carmine Arroyo, spent much of his childhood. Every Christmas, New Year's, and Three Kings Day, Carmine's extended family would get together in his hometown, Bayamón, to celebrate together, and his grandmother would bring a cake big enough to feed everyone. Our version of this classic uses a chocolate sponge cake, which is soaked with a mix of condensed milk, evaporated milk, and heavy cream—the "three milks" in the name—and then topped with sweet, creamy dulce de leche (the fourth "milk" in the recipe) for additional flavor.

Cake

¾ cup all-purpose flour

½ cup unsweetened Dutch-process cocoa powder

10 extra-large eggs

1 cup plus 2 tablespoons granulated sugar

2 tablespoons pure vanilla extract

Vegetable oil spray

Three Milk "Soak"

14 ounces condensed milk

12 ounces evaporated milk

1 cup heavy cream

1 tablespoon pure vanilla extract

To Assemble

16 ounces dulce de leche, homemade (see page 58) or store-bought

recipe continues on the next page

Make the Cake

1. Preheat the oven to 350°F. In a small bowl, whisk together the flour and cocoa powder; set aside. In the bowl of a stand mixer fitted with the whisk attachment, whip the eggs and sugar together for 2 minutes on medium, then add the vanilla and whip on high until the mixture has tripled in volume, 6 to 8 minutes. Remove the bowl from the mixer, add the dry ingredients, and use a rubber spatula to fold and mix everything together until the mixture no longer has streaks, making sure to scrape down the sides and bottom of the bowl.

....

When "folding" ingredients together in any recipe, don't be afraid to mix until the ingredients are completely combined. The folding motion is gentler than a regular mixing motion, but everything still needs to be well combined.

....

2. Spray a 9 x 13-inch casserole dish with vegetable oil spray and pour the batter into the prepared dish. Bake for 45 to 50 minutes, until a paring knife inserted into the center of the cake comes out clean. Let cool to room temperature; the cake will deflate a bit as it cools. When the cake has cooled, use a paring knife to poke it all over, 30 to 40 times.

Soak the Cake

In a medium bowl, mix the condensed milk, evaporated milk, cream, and vanilla, then pour the mixture over the cake, distributing the liquid as evenly as possible over the cake's surface. Cover the casserole dish with plastic wrap and refrigerate the cake for at least 4 hours, preferably overnight, so that the liquid can soak into the cake.

Assemble the Cake

Heat the dulce de leche on the stove or in the microwave until it is fluid. Uncover the cake and pour the dulce de leche over the top as evenly as possible; use a small offset spatula or rubber spatula to spread it around and even it out. Refrigerate the cake for 30 minutes to let the dulce de leche firm up before serving. ★

Make Ahead

The finished cake can be wrapped in the casserole dish and kept in the refrigerator for 3 to 4 days, though it may become soggy and hard to cut into clean pieces after 2 days.

Above and Beyond
Dulce de Leche

Remove the label from an unopened 16-ounce can of sweetened condensed milk, place the can in a saucepan, and add water to cover the can by at least 1 inch. Bring the water to a boil over high heat, then continue to boil the can for 2 hours, making sure that there is always enough water in the saucepan to cover the can by at least 1 inch. (If the can does not remain covered by water it may over heat, which can cause it to burst.) Remove the can from the water and allow it to cool completely before opening it. ★

Spiced Molten Chocolate Cakes

Makes 8 individual cakes plus 1 test cake

The molten chocolate cake, like many great desserts, was the result of a delicious accident. In 1987, Jean-Georges Vongerichten, chef and co-owner of Jean-Georges restaurant in New York, was playing with a recipe for a tiny, delicate chocolate cake. When he baked the cake in a larger size, he discovered that the center didn't cook all the way through, and the molten chocolate cake was born. Or so the story goes. Like most great origin myths, this story has been disputed. But whether it's true or not, this little cake became an instant classic. By the late '90s, it seemed like every restaurant in the city had a molten chocolate cake on the dessert menu.

Our version is based on Jean-Georges's original recipe, but we add some of the same spices that are in our spiced hot cocoa: some cinnamon, a pinch of cloves, and just enough ancho chile to give the whole thing a touch of spiciness that builds on your tongue as you eat the cake, bite by bite. Pictured on page 22.

5 extra-large eggs

5 extra-large egg yolks

½ cup plus 2 tablespoons granulated sugar

5¼ teaspoons all-purpose flour

1 tablespoon ancho chile powder

1 teaspoon ground cinnamon

¼ teaspoon ground cloves

10 ounces dark chocolate (preferably 60% cacao), coarsely chopped

1¼ cups (2½ sticks) unsalted butter

Vegetable oil spray

Special Tools

9 (4-ounce) foil ramekins (see page 17)

1. In a large bowl, whisk together the eggs, egg yolks, and sugar until the mixture looks fairly homogenous; set aside. In a small bowl, mix together the flour, chile powder, cinnamon, and cloves; set aside.

2. Melt the chocolate and butter together in the top of a double boiler, stirring to keep the chocolate from burning, or microwave them together in 10- to 20-second intervals, stirring after each interval, until they become liquid. Whisk the butter and chocolate briskly until combined. Pour the warm chocolate mixture into the egg mixture and whisk well until everything is combined and there are no visible streaks. Add the flour mixture and whisk gently until there are no clumps.

3. Coat the insides of nine 4-ounce foil ramekins with vegetable oil spray. Use a pastry bag, ladle, or ice cream scoop to divide the batter evenly among the ramekins (they will be almost full). Set the ramekins on a sheet pan or in a casserole dish and wrap the entire thing with plastic wrap. Refrigerate for at least 4 hours, preferably overnight.

4. When the cakes are cold, bake one to test the baking time for your oven. Preheat the oven to 425°F. Remove one filled ramekin from the refrigerator, unwrap it, and bake it for 15 minutes. (The cake should no longer have a visibly wet spot on the top when done.) Insert a thermometer into the center to make sure the temperature is at least 160°F, then immediately flip it out onto a serving plate and cut into it; the very center of the cake should be liquid. If the cake is undercooked, add 1 to 2 minutes to the baking time; if it's overcooked, reduce the baking time by 1 to 2 minutes. The remaining cakes should be removed from the refrigerator and baked just before serving. ★

recipe continues on the next page

Make Ahead

The unbaked cakes can be kept in their ramekins in the refrigerator for 3 to 4 days.

Serving Suggestion

Caramel Sauce (page 162) and Vanilla Ice Cream (page 157).

 tip

The easiest way to portion this sticky, liquid batter is to use a pastry bag (see "Using a Pastry Bag," page 108).

Chocolate Glaze

The key to making a glaze with a smooth, rather than grainy, texture is to let the hot cream sit on the chocolate until the chocolate melts on its own, rather than trying to hurry it by whisking or stirring.

14 ounces dark chocolate (preferably 55% cacao), coarsely chopped

1½ cups heavy cream

½ cup light corn syrup

Put the chocolate in a medium heatproof bowl; set aside. In a small saucepan, bring the cream and corn syrup to a boil over high heat, stirring occasionally. Pour the cream mixture over the chocolate and let it sit until the chocolate has melted, about 5 minutes, then whisk the ingredients together until the glaze is smooth. Let the glaze cool until it is still warm and fluid but not hot. ★

Make Ahead

This glaze can be refrigerated for up to 2 weeks. Reheat it in the microwave in 30-second intervals, stirring after each interval, or by putting the container of glaze in a bowl of hot water until it is fluid.

**Contruction
Instructions**

Chocolate Mousse Cake

Makes one 9-inch cake

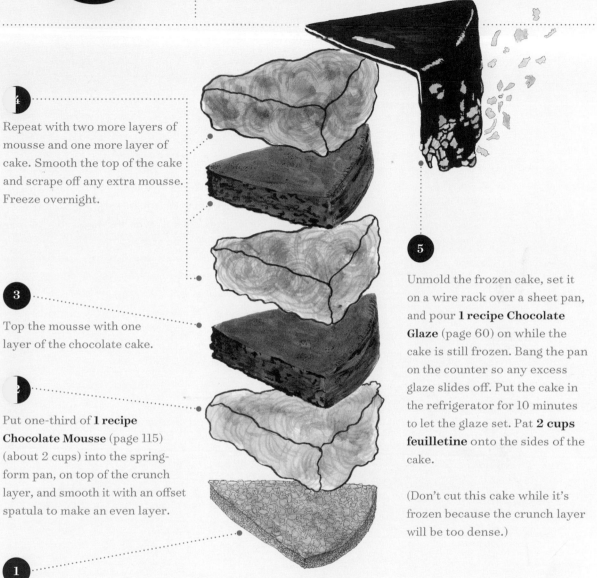

4

Repeat with two more layers of mousse and one more layer of cake. Smooth the top of the cake and scrape off any extra mousse. Freeze overnight.

3

Top the mousse with one layer of the chocolate cake.

2

Put one-third of **1 recipe Chocolate Mousse** (page 115) (about 2 cups) into the spring-form pan, on top of the crunch layer, and smooth it with an offset spatula to make an even layer.

5

Unmold the frozen cake, set it on a wire rack over a sheet pan, and pour **1 recipe Chocolate Glaze** (page 60) on while the cake is still frozen. Bang the pan on the counter so any excess glaze slides off. Put the cake in the refrigerator for 10 minutes to let the glaze set. Pat **2 cups feuilletine** onto the sides of the cake.

(Don't cut this cake while it's frozen because the crunch layer will be too dense.)

1

Crunch Layer: Melt **8 ounces coarsely chopped milk chocolate** in the top of a double boiler, stirring to keep the chocolate from burning, or microwave in 20-second intervals, stirring after each interval, until liquid. Remove from the heat and stir in **2 tablespoons vegetable oil**, **a pinch of salt**, and ¾ **cup feuilletine** (see page 132).

Pour the mixture into the bottom of a **9-inch springform pan with 3-inch-tall sides** (see page 17). Spread evenly and freeze. (You can also make this in a 2½-inch-deep springform pan, but you'll have leftover mousse.) Cut the domed top off **1 (8-inch) layer of chocolate cake** (page 29) and cut the cake horizontally to make two layers. (For the easiest way to get even layers, see "How to Assemble and Frost a Perfect, Showstopping Cake," page 24.)

**Chocolate Canoes
with Vanilla Cream Filling**
recipe on page 85

Whoopie Pies
recipe on page 83

baked goods

How to Whip up Butter, Cream & Eggs

Most of our recipes contain instructions to whip or beat something—cream, butter, egg whites, or egg yolks—in a stand mixer. This whipping or beating is often the most important part of the recipe. If you do this step correctly, you'll get fluffy cakes, chewy cookies with crisp edges, smooth, airy mousses, and fluffy whipped cream. So what, exactly, do we mean when we say to whip something to "soft" or "stiff" peaks? What constitutes a "fluffy" butter-and-sugar mixture? How will you know when egg yolks "form ribbons"? Here are our guidelines for whipping it all up.

Creaming Butter

Most of our cake and cookie recipes say to cream butter and sugar for at least 3 minutes. While the butter might look "light and fluffy" after only a minute or so, it's important to keep going for the full time specified in the recipe. When you beat butter and sugar together for long enough, the sugar will begin to dissolve into the butter and the mixture will look less grainy and have a smoother texture.

Whipped Cream

When you whip cream, there are two key things to remember:

The cream should always be as cold as possible. This helps the fat in the cream stay firm so that it absorbs air properly.

You should always whip cream at a medium speed. This gives the cream time to absorb a lot of air so that it will be fluffy and voluminous.

How can you tell when the cream is ready? Here's what to look for:

Soft Peaks

You'll know you've reached this stage when the cream begins to hold its shape in the bowl and you start to see ridges, like a range of low hills, forming in the cream. If you stop the mixer and pull the whisk out, the cream will come to a point but will then fall back into itself rather than holding its shape.

Medium Peaks

When the ridges in the cream start to deepen and hold their shape, you've reached the medium peak stage. When the whisk is removed, it will form a peak that will almost hold its shape, but the tip of the peak will collapse onto itself.

Stiff Peaks

You'll be able to tell you've reached stiff peak stage even before you turn off the mixer because the long ridges in the cream will suddenly become shorter and look more like clumps. When you pull the whisk out of the cream, it will leave a short, pointy peak. (Don't beat the cream any further or it will start to turn into butter.)

Whipped Egg Whites

Whipping egg whites is similar to whipping cream, except that you will always need to add sugar to the egg whites if you want them to hold their shape. (Without sugar, egg whites aren't stable enough to stay stiff.) When you whip egg whites, there are two key things to remember:

Egg whites should always be at room temperature when you whip them. This will help their proteins break down more quickly and allow them to absorb air.

Egg whites should always be whipped at medium speed so they can incorporate as much air as possible and build volume before they become stiff.

How can you tell when egg whites are ready? Here's what to look for:

Frothy

If you're just whisking egg whites to break them up a little, you'll want to whisk them to become very light and loose and bubbly so there's not a big pool of liquid at the bottom of the bowl.

Soft Peaks

When the whites transform from frothy bubbles to a white mass that looks slightly sticky, you've reached soft peak stage. If you stop the mixer and pull the whisk out, the whites should come to a point but then collapse back into the bowl.

Stiff Peaks

When the surface of the egg whites looks glossy and shiny, you've reached stiff peak stage. When you pull the whisk out of the whites, it will leave a pointy peak. (Don't beat the egg whites any further or the chemical bonds holding everything together will break, and the eggs' liquids and solids will separate.)

Whipped Egg Yolks

When you whip egg yolks with sugar, the goal is to dissolve the sugar so that the mixture is smooth instead of grainy. To get the best results, egg yolks should always be room temperature when you whip them; this will help their proteins break down more quickly. Unlike egg whites, yolks can be whipped at high speed.

When you whip yolks and sugar together, you want the mixture to "form ribbons." This means that when you stop the mixer and let the yolk fall from the whisk into the bowl, a line of yolk should sit on top of the pool of liquid for a second before settling into it.

Chocolate Stout Gingerbread

Makes two 8½ x 4½-inch loaves

This rich, flavorful gingerbread was inspired by our friends at Brooklyn Brewery and their Black Chocolate Stout, the very first beer their brewmaster, Garrett Oliver, developed for them. This moist, fragrant gingerbread doesn't have any actual chocolate in it—its flavor comes from adding a healthy pour of the chocolaty beer to the batter. Because the stout is only sold in the fall and winter months, we held an event called The Arrival of the Chocolate Stout; Garrett came to the café to talk to our customers about the beer, and we served the bread warm with freshly whipped cream and a pint of the stout on the side. It was an utterly perfect fall combination.

¾ cup chocolate stout (preferably Brooklyn Brewery Black Chocolate Stout)

1 cup unsulfured molasses

¼ cup water

½ teaspoon baking soda

Vegetable oil spray

2 cups all-purpose flour

1½ teaspoons baking powder

2 tablespoons ground ginger

1 teaspoon ground cinnamon

¼ teaspoon freshly grated nutmeg

⅛ teaspoon ground cardamom

3 extra-large eggs

1 cup dark brown sugar

1 cup granulated sugar

¾ cup vegetable oil

Special Tools

Two 1-pound (8½ x 4½-inch) loaf pans

1. In a medium saucepan, whisk together the chocolate stout, molasses, and water. Bring the mixture to a boil over high heat, then remove the pan from the heat and whisk in the baking soda. (This will cause the mixture to rise a few inches momentarily.) Let the mixture cool to room temperature, then pour it into a large liquid measuring cup and add water until there is exactly 2 cups of liquid.

2. Preheat the oven to 350°F. Spray the sides and bottoms of two 8½ x 4½-inch loaf pans with vegetable oil spray, line the bottoms with parchment paper, and spray the top of the parchment.

3. Sift the flour, baking powder, and spices into a medium bowl; set aside. In the bowl of a stand mixer fitted with the whisk attachment, mix together the eggs and both sugars on medium until the ingredients are well combined and there are no lumps left, about 30 seconds, then use a rubber spatula to scrape down the sides and bottom of the bowl and whisk again for a few seconds until well combined.

4. Turn the mixer to low and add the oil and then the beer mixture. Add the flour mixture in two batches, whisking on low after each addition until the ingredients are just combined and there are no lumps of dry ingredients left. Scrape down the sides of the bowl, then whisk for a few more seconds to eliminate any clumps. Divide the batter between the prepared loaf pans.

5. Bake the bread for 50 to 60 minutes, until a paring knife inserted into the center of each loaf comes out moist but with no more than a couple of crumbs sticking to it. ★

Make Ahead
The gingerbread can wrapped in two layers of plastic wrap and kept at room temperature for up to 3 days or frozen for up to 2 weeks.

Brownies

Makes 24 brownies

When we first started planning the menu for The Chocolate Room, we knew that we needed to serve a brownie. It couldn't be just any brownie, though—it had to be a brownie so good that we'd never want to try another kind ever again. We love both cakey and chewy types, so we opted to combine the two and landed on what we think is the perfect combination. Light and cakey but also rich and moist, these brownies are our ideal. (They're also the perfect base for our Brownie Sundae, page 87.) There is one trick to making these brownies: their texture depends on the use of Belcolade chocolate. Depending on the brand of chocolate you buy, you may end up with brownies that are lighter or denser than the ones we make in the café. But however they turn out, they will be delicious.

Vegetable oil spray

2 cups cake flour

¾ cup unsweetened Dutch-process cocoa powder

2 teaspoons baking powder

8 extra-large eggs

1 tablespoon pure vanilla extract

½ teaspoon salt

12 ounces dark chocolate (preferably 60% cacao), coarsely chopped

2 cups (4 sticks) unsalted butter

3¾ cups granulated sugar

1. Preheat the oven to 350°F. Coat the bottom and sides of a deep-sided sheet pan or a 12 x 16-inch baking pan with vegetable oil spray, line the bottom with parchment paper, and spray the top of the parchment.

2. Sift the cake flour, cocoa powder, and baking powder into a large bowl. In a medium bowl, combine the eggs, vanilla, and salt and whisk vigorously to combine. Set both bowls aside.

3. Melt the chocolate and butter together in the top of a double boiler, stirring to keep the chocolate from burning, or microwave them together in 30-second intervals, stirring after each interval, until they become liquid. Whisk the chocolate and butter briskly until combined.

4. Put the sugar into a large bowl, then pour the melted chocolate mixture over it and whisk to combine. Add half the flour mixture to the bowl and whisk gently; repeat with the remaining flour mixture. Add the egg mixture to the bowl and care-fully fold all the ingredients together with a rubber spatula, scraping down the sides and bottom of the bowl, just until all the ingredients are fully combined.

5. Pour the batter into the prepared pan and smooth the top with a small offset spatula or a rubber spatula. If there are streaks of egg visible on the top of the batter, use the spatula to smooth them into the batter in a circular motion. Bake the brownies for 40 minutes, until the batter has risen a bit, the brownies have an even, slightly bubbling crust, and the edges are starting to dry out and break a bit. Let the brownies cool completely in the pan set on a wire rack before slicing and serving. ★

Make Ahead
The brownies will keep in the refrigerator, uncut and wrapped in two layers of plastic wrap, for ten days, or for up to six weeks in the freezer. The cut brownies can be stored in an airtight container at room temperature for 2 to 3 days.

Dark Chocolate Walnut Cookies
recipe on page 74

Chocolate Chip Cookies
recipe opposite

Milk Chocolate Peanut Butter Sea Salt Cookies
recipe on page 72

Chocolate Chip Cookies

Makes about 36 cookies

Back in 2005, when we first opened our doors at The Chocolate Room, we used to sell two different kinds of chocolate chip cookies: one was a soft, cakey cookie, and the other was a thin, crisp cookie. We loved them both, but it became clear very quickly that the softer one was by far the more popular of the two. These days we serve just one version of the cookie, with a slightly chewy center, crispy edges, and a very generous helping of chocolate chunks. We make these cookies in huge batches, and they fly out the door almost as fast as we can make them.

3⅓ cups all-purpose flour

¾ teaspoon baking soda

1½ teaspoons salt

3 extra-large eggs

1 tablespoon pure vanilla extract

1½ cups (3 sticks) unsalted butter, at room temperature

¾ cup granulated sugar

2 cups dark brown sugar

20 ounces dark chocolate (preferably 60% cacao), coarsely chopped to about the size of chocolate chips

Special Tool

1½-ounce (3-tablespoon) cookie scoop (optional, see page 19)

Instead of cutting up the chocolate by hand, you can chop it by pulsing it in a food processor. Make sure each pulse is very short, so that the machine doesn't heat up and start to melt the chocolate. (Taking a little of the flour from the batter recipe and adding it to the chocolate will also help keep it from becoming a paste.)

1. In a medium bowl, mix together the flour, baking soda, and salt; set aside. Put the eggs and the vanilla in a small bowl; set aside.

2. In the bowl of a stand mixer fitted with the paddle attachment, combine the butter and both sugars and mix on low until the ingredients begin to come together. Raise the mixer speed to medium-high and mix for 3 minutes. Stop the mixer and use a rubber spatula to scrape down the sides and bottom of the bowl.

3. With the mixer on low, add the eggs and vanilla, letting the eggs slide in one at a time; mix on low until the ingredients are just combined. Scrape down the sides and bottom of the mixing bowl, then beat the mixture on high for 1 minute, until it is smooth and homogenous and a little fluffy. Add the flour mixture to the bowl and mix on low until just incorporated. Scrape down the sides and bottom of the bowl and mix for 10 seconds to combine. Add the chopped chocolate and mix on low until just incorporated, about 10 seconds.

4. Remove the bowl and use a rubber spatula to scrape down the sides and bottom of the bowl, then finish mixing everything by hand to ensure there are no pockets of unincorporated ingredients.

5. Transfer the cookie dough to a medium bowl and refrigerate for at least 4 hours and preferably overnight, so that the cookies will hold their shape when baked.

recipe continues on the next page

6. Preheat the oven to 375°F. Line two sheet pans with parchment paper or silicone liners. Use a tablespoon or a 1½-ounce (3-tablespoon) cookie scoop to form balls of the dough, each about 1¾ inches in diameter, and set them on the sheet pans about 1½ inches apart. (Fill the cookie scoop or tablespoon generously and use a hand to round the excess dough so each portion is formed into a ball.) You should be able to fit 12 cookies on each sheet.

7. Bake for 15 minutes. The cookies will spread out, the edges will brown slightly, and the centers of the cookies will be set but soft. Remove from the oven and let cool completely on the pans. ★

Make Ahead

The cookie dough can be refrigerated for 4 to 5 days or frozen for up to 1 month. The baked cookies will stay fresh in an airtight container at room temperature for up to 3 days.

Milk Chocolate Peanut Butter Sea Salt Cookies

Makes about 30 cookies

This recipe started as a wonderful mistake. Our former chef Jennifer Jupiter had planned to make regular peanut butter cookies, but somehow the proportions got mixed up, and she didn't add enough flour to the recipe. She baked the cookies anyway and found that the result was even more delicious than the cookies she had meant to make. They were moist instead of dry, tender instead of sandy. They were decadent. And our customers fell in love with them. Every day for months after we unveiled them our regulars would come rushing into the store in the afternoon, worried that we'd run out. The batter for these cookies can be a bit tricky to work with because it is wet and oily and needs to be chilled so that it will hold its shape when it's scooped, but the result is definitely worth the little bit of extra effort. Pictured on page 70.

½ cup vegetable oil

1½ teaspoons pure vanilla extract

1 extra-large egg

1¼ cups all-purpose flour

1 teaspoon baking powder

½ teaspoon baking soda

½ teaspoon salt

5 tablespoons unsalted butter, at room temperature

½ cup plus 2 tablespoons dark brown sugar

¾ cup confectioners' sugar

½ cup natural creamy peanut butter with salt

6 ounces milk chocolate, coarsely chopped to about the size of chocolate chips

Fleur de sel, for sprinkling

Special Tool

½-ounce (1-tablespoon) cookie scoop (optional, see page 19)

1. In a medium bowl, mix together the oil, vanilla, and egg. In a large bowl, mix together the flour, baking powder, baking soda, and salt; set both bowls aside.

2. In the bowl of a stand mixer fitted with the paddle attachment, cream the butter and both sugars on medium-low speed until very light and fluffy, about 3 minutes. Add the peanut butter and mix on medium-low until incorporated, about 10 seconds, then use a rubber spatula to scrape down the sides and bottom of the bowl.

....

 tip

If your peanut butter has separated and the oil is floating above the solids, you can put the entire contents of the jar into your stand mixer and mix it until it is smooth, then measure out the amount required for the cookies.

....

3. With the mixer on low, add the oil mixture in a slow stream and mix until fully incorporated.

4. Scrape down the sides and bottom of the bowl, add the flour mixture, and mix on low speed until just incorporated, then scrape down the sides and bottom of the bowl. Remove the bowl, add the chocolate, and mix everything together with a rubber spatula. Scoop the batter into a medium bowl and cover tightly with plastic wrap. Refrigerate the dough for at least 2 hours, preferably overnight.

5. Preheat the oven to 350°F. Line two sheet pans with parchment paper or silicone liners. Use a tablespoon or a ½-ounce (1-tablespoon) cookie scoop to form balls of dough, measuring out one flat tablespoon's worth of dough for each. Cup the dough for each cookie in your hand lightly to shape it into a ball, and place the cookies 2 to 3 inches apart on the pans. You should be able to fit about 12 cookies on each sheet. Sprinkle each cookie with a small pinch of fleur de sel.

6. Freeze the cookies on the pans for 15 minutes, then bake for 15 minutes. When the cookies are done, they will still be very soft and tender, but their edges will be starting to crisp. Set them aside on the pans for a few minutes to firm up, then transfer to a wire rack to finish cooling. Repeat until all the batter has been used. ★

Make Ahead

The cookie dough can be refrigerated for 4 to 5 days or frozen for up to 1 month. The baked cookies will stay fresh in an airtight container at room temperature for up to 3 days.

Dark Chocolate Walnut Cookies

Makes about 20 cookies

These rich cookies are more like brownies than regular cookies. In fact, when we created these, we thought of them as a stand-in for a nut-filled version of our delicious brownies. The process for making them is also similar to the process for our brownies: we mix melted butter and chocolate directly into the dough (which gives the cookies a soft, fudgy texture), and then we add even more chocolate and walnuts. There's also a touch of espresso powder in the mix, which gives the whole thing an extra-rich flavor (and a little bit of a kick). Pictured on page 70.

6 ounces dark chocolate (preferably 60% cacao), coarsely chopped

½ cup chopped walnuts

¼ cup all-purpose flour

¼ teaspoon baking powder

¼ teaspoon salt

4 tablespoons (½ stick) unsalted butter

2 ounces unsweetened chocolate (preferably 100% cacao), coarsely chopped

2 extra-large eggs

¾ cup granulated sugar

2 teaspoons instant espresso powder

1 teaspoon pure vanilla extract

1. Preheat the oven to 350°F. Line two sheet pans with parchment paper or silicone liners. In a small bowl, mix together 3 ounces of the dark chocolate and the walnuts. In a medium bowl, mix together the flour, baking powder, and salt. Set both bowls aside.

2. Melt the butter, the remaining 3 ounces of dark chocolate, and the unsweetened chocolate together in the top of a double boiler, stirring to keep the chocolate from burning, or microwave them together in 10- to 20-second intervals, stirring after each interval, until they become liquid. Whisk the butter and chocolate briskly until combined. Set aside.

3. In the bowl of a stand mixer fitted with the whisk attachment, whip the eggs, sugar, instant espresso, and vanilla together on medium-low until the mixture comes together, then whip on high for 12 minutes; the mixture will nearly triple in volume. Turn the mixer to low and slowly pour the melted chocolate mixture in; mix until just incorporated.

4. Remove the bowl from the mixer, add the chopped chocolate and nuts to the dough, and fold everything together with a rubber spatula until just incorporated. Add half the flour mixture to the bowl and fold it into the batter until it is just incorporated, then repeat with the remaining flour mixture, scraping down the sides and bottom of the bowl to ensure that all the ingredients are evenly incorporated.

5. Use a tablespoon or a 1-ounce (1-tablespoon) cookie scoop to portion out the batter, using about 2 tablespoons of batter per cookie, and place the cookies about 2 inches apart on the prepared pans. You should be able to fit 12 cookies on each sheet. Bake for 12 minutes, then let the cookies cool completely on the pans. To remove them from the pans, run a small offset spatula or a thin knife between the cookies and the parchment paper or liner. ★

Make Ahead

The cookie dough can be refrigerated for 4 to 5 days or frozen for up to 1 month. The baked cookies will stay fresh in an airtight container at room temperature for up to 3 days.

Chocolate Sandwich Cookies

Makes about 30 cookies

In the world of American treats, there is nothing more iconic than the chocolate sandwich cookie. This fairly simple food—a pair of chocolate wafer cookies with creamy filling between them—probably conjures up more childhood nostalgia than all the pies and cakes in the world. The first commercially produced sandwich cookie was the Hydrox, introduced on January 1, 1910, followed by the now classic Oreo in March 1912.

Our chocolate sandwich cookies have their own unique combination of textures and flavors. The cookies have a rich cocoa flavor and an exceptionally crisp texture, and the filling is a delicious white chocolate butter cream. We suggest chilling the filled cookies after you assemble them to keep the filling firm. (In fact, we've found that they're particularly delicious when eaten directly from the refrigerator.)

Cookies

1⅓ cups unsweetened Dutch-process cocoa powder

1½ cups all-purpose flour

¼ teaspoon salt

1 cup (2 sticks) unsalted butter, at room temperature

2¼ cups granulated sugar

2 extra-large eggs

1 teaspoon pure vanilla extract

Filling

1 cup (2 sticks) unsalted butter, at room temperature

6 ounces white chocolate, coarsely chopped

1 extra-large egg

1 extra-large egg white

¼ teaspoon pure vanilla extract

¼ teaspoon salt

½ cup granulated sugar

2 tablespoons water

1 teaspoon light corn syrup

Special Tool

2¼-inch ring cutter (see page 21)

Make the Cookies

1. Sift together the cocoa powder, flour, and salt into a medium bowl and set aside. In the bowl of a stand mixer fitted with the paddle attachment, cream the butter and sugar on medium until the mixture is very light and fluffy, about 3 minutes. Use a rubber spatula to scrape down the sides and bottom of the bowl. Add the eggs and vanilla and beat on medium until incorporated, about 10 seconds. Beat on high for 1 minute to incorporate a bit of air. Scrape down the sides and bottom of the bowl.

2. Add one-third of the flour mixture and mix on low until just incorporated, about 20 seconds, then scrape down the sides and bottom of the bowl. Repeat twice more to incorporate the remaining flour mixture. Remove the bowl from the mixer and finish mixing by hand, using a rubber spatula in a beating motion, scraping down the sides and bottom of the bowl to ensure that all the ingredients are evenly incorporated.

3. Divide the dough into thirds, press it into round disks, and place each disk between two sheets of parchment paper. Working with one disk at a time, roll the dough out until it is ⅛ inch thick. Freeze the rolled dough until it has firmed up, at least 30 minutes.

recipe continues on the next page

4. Preheat the oven to 350°F. Line two sheet pans with parchment paper. Remove the dough from the freezer, remove the top sheet of parchment, and use a 2¼-inch ring cutter to cut as many cookies as you can (about 20 per sheet of dough). Transfer the cookies to the prepared pans, leaving about ½ inch between them. If the dough becomes too soft as you work, put it back in the freezer to harden up. Bake for 10 minutes, until the cookies are crisp, then let the cookies cool completely on the pans.

Make the Filling

1. Cut the butter into slices ¼ to ½ inch thick and set them aside. Melt the white chocolate in the top of a double boiler, stirring to keep it from burning, or microwave it in 10-second intervals, stirring after each interval, until it becomes liquid. Cover the bowl to keep the chocolate warm and set aside.

2. In the bowl of a stand mixer fitted with the whisk attachment, combine the egg, egg white, vanilla, and salt and whip together on medium until the egg is frothy, about 2 minutes. Turn the mixer to low and let it continue to run.

3. In a small saucepan, combine the sugar, water, and corn syrup and bring to a boil over high heat, stirring occasionally. When the mixture starts to boil vigorously, let it boil for exactly 1 minute. With the mixer on medium, slowly pour the sugar syrup into the egg mixture in a thin, steady stream about the width of pencil, making sure not to pour it onto the sides of the bowl, where it would stick and solidify. Turn the mixer to high and whip everything together until the sides of the mixing bowl have cooled to room temperature, about 3 minutes.

If the sugar syrup sticks to the side of the mixing bowl, you can use a kitchen torch to heat the outside of the bowl until the sugar is hot enough to slide down into the rest of the mixture.

4. Turn the mixer to low and drop the pieces of butter into the mixer one at a time, waiting 10 seconds between each piece. As the butter is added, the mixture will begin to thicken and look curdled. When all the butter has been added, turn the mixer to high and whisk for 30 seconds.

5. Check the temperature of the melted chocolate to make sure that it's lukewarm; if it's no longer fluid, reheat it a bit, but make sure that it's not too hot. With the mixer on low, slowly pour the chocolate into the butter mixture, then mix on medium until incorporated. (The heat of the chocolate will melt the butter just a little and will smooth out the filling's appearance.) Turn the mixer to high and whip for 1 minute to make the filling fluffy.

Assemble the Cookies

Working with one cookie at a time, put a little less than 1 tablespoon of filling onto the center of the flat side of the cookie. Place another cookie on top of the filling and gently press the cookies together until the filling has just reached the edges of the cookie sandwich. Repeat with the remaining cookies, then refrigerate them for at least 1 hour to firm up the filling before serving. ★

To get a really even, clean layer of filling in between the cookies, put the filling into a pastry bag and pipe a layer ½ inch thick in the center of cookie, leaving a ¼ inch border of cookie bare. Top it with a second cookie and press the filling down until it comes almost to the edge of the sandwich.

recipe continues on the next page

Make Ahead

The dough for the wafer cookies can be refrigerated for up to 2 weeks or frozen for up to 1 month. The baked cookies can be kept in an airtight container at room temperature for up to 3 days. The buttercream can be refrigerated for up to 10 days or frozen for up to 1 month. The assembled cookies can be kept in the refrigerator for 2 to 3 days.

Above and Beyond
Chocolate Cookie Crumbs

When we make these cookies, we bake the scraps and turn them into crumbs to use in other recipes. If you need just the crumbs, however, you can make them without making the cookies:

Make a half-batch of the cookie dough in the recipe above (using half of the ingredients listed). Preheat the oven to 350°F. Place the cookie dough between two sheets of parchment paper, press the dough into a flat disk, then roll it out until it is about ⅛ inch thick. Peel off the top piece of parchment and place the bottom piece with the rolled-out dough on it on a sheet pan. Bake for 15 minutes, then let cool to room temperature. When the giant cookie has cooled, break it up with your hands, transfer to a food processor, and pulse until it forms fine crumbs. ★

Chocolate-Dipped Coconut Macaroons

Makes about 20 macaroons

These big, chewy macaroons are particularly popular around Passover because they don't contain any wheat or other grains. We make them with a combination of sweetened and unsweetened coconut mixed with a generous amount of coconut cream; the combination gives them a rich, nuanced coconut flavor and helps them develop a crispy, caramelized exterior. (While we don't usually like to use ingredients with stabilizers, we always use Coco Lopez coconut cream in these macaroons because it keeps them from falling apart when they're dipped in chocolate.) Pictured on page 80.

3 cups unsweetened shredded coconut

2¾ cups sweetened shredded coconut

1 cup sweetened cream of coconut (ideally Coco Lopez brand)

2 tablespoons light corn syrup

4 extra-large egg whites

1½ teaspoons pure vanilla extract

½ teaspoon salt

16 ounces dark chocolate (preferably 60% cacao)

Special Tool

1½-ounce (3-tablespoon) cookie scoop (optional, see page 19)

tip

If you can't find finely shredded coconut, use a food processor to grind larger flakes into smaller pieces.

1. In a large bowl, mix together the two types of coconut; set aside. In a medium bowl, whisk together the cream of coconut, corn syrup, egg whites, and vanilla extract until combined. Add the mixture to the coconut and mix everything together by hand, kneading the coconut so that all of the liquid is distributed evenly. Refrigerate the mixture for a minimum of 6 hours, preferably overnight, so that the coconut soaks up the liquid and the mixture firms up.

2. Preheat the oven to 375°F. Line two sheet pans with parchment paper. Use your hands or a 1½-ounce (3-tablespoon) cookie scoop to form tightly packed balls of the coconut mixture, each about 1¾ inches in diameter. (If you're using a cookie scoop, fill the scoop but pack the mixture down so that you form a flat bottom for the macaroons; if you're using your hands, press the balls down onto the parchment paper to create a flat bottom.) The macaroons should be packed very tightly so they won't fall apart when they bake. Set them about ½ inch apart on the prepared pan.

3. Bake for 10 minutes, then rotate the pans so that the macaroons on the lower rack move to the top for even browning and bake for 10 minutes more. The macaroons should be a dark golden brown and have bits of dark brown where the shreds of coconut have caramelized. Let cool completely.

4. Line two sheet pans with parchment paper. Temper the chocolate using any of the tempering techniques listed on page 126, then bring it back to working temperature. When the chocolate is ready, dip each macaroon so that one side is completely enrobed in chocolate, shake it a bit to let the excess chocolate fall back into the bowl, then set it on one of the prepared pans. When all the macaroons have been dipped, set the pans aside in a cool, dry place to let the chocolate set. ★

Make Ahead
The coconut mixture can be kept in the refrigerator for up to 10 days. The baked, chocolate-dipped macaroons can be stored in an airtight container at room temperature for up to 1 week.

Above and Beyond
Mini Macaroons
To make tiny mini macaroons, like the ones we use for our Fondue (page 122), scoop the batter with a ½-ounce (1-tablespoon) scoop and bake for 25 minutes, rotating the sheet pans halfway through the baking time. The recipe will make 60 mini macaroons. ★

Chocolate-Dipped Coconut Macaroons
recipe on page 78

Chocolate-Dipped Graham Crackers

recipe on page 82

Chocolate-Dipped Graham Crackers

Makes about 25 cookies

Graham crackers, which were invented in the early nineteenth century as a health food, were originally made with a type of whole wheat flour called graham flour, but over the past two hundred years, the cookies have evolved into a beloved sweet. Our homemade graham crackers, flavored with honey, vanilla, and cinnamon, are dense, rich, and infinitely more flavorful than supermarket versions. The cookies are made out of a delicate short dough, like a pie crust dough. Pieces of butter in the dough create steam as they bake, giving the finished cookies their crisp texture. Once the cookies have baked, we give them a smooth coat of chocolate. At the cafés, we sell versions dipped in semisweet chocolate, which contrasts with the cookies' sweetness, and milk chocolate, which reminds us of campfire s'mores and other childhood treats. Pictured on page 81.

7 tablespoons unsalted butter, cold

⅓ cup whole milk

6 tablespoons honey

2 tablespoons pure vanilla extract

3 cups all-purpose flour, plus extra for dusting

1¼ cups light brown sugar

1 teaspoon baking soda

1 teaspoon salt

½ teaspoon ground cinnamon

24 ounces dark chocolate (ideally 70% cacao) or milk chocolate

1. Cut the butter into even squares, about ½ x ½ inch, and set aside in the refrigerator. In a small bowl, whisk together the milk, honey, and vanilla; set aside.

2. In the bowl of a stand mixer fitted with the paddle attachment, mix together the flour, brown sugar, baking soda, salt, and cinnamon on low until combined, about 30 seconds. Turn off the mixer and sift through the mixture with your fingers, breaking up any remaining clumps of brown sugar, then mix for a few seconds to combine.

3. Add the cold butter and beat on low until the mixture is mealy and the remaining pieces of butter are no bigger than small lentils. With the mixer on low, pour in the milk mixture in a slow, steady stream; mix until the dough just comes together. Divide the dough in half and shape it into flat disks. Wrap the dough in two layers of plastic wrap and refrigerate for at least 4 hours, preferably overnight.

4. Remove one dough disk, unwrap it, and set it on a lightly floured piece of parchment paper. Lightly flour the top of the dough, cover it with a second piece of parchment, and roll the dough out into a rectangle about ¼ inch thick. Freeze the dough for 20 to 30 minutes to firm up. Repeat with the second disk of dough.

5. Preheat the oven to 350°F. Line three sheet pans with parchment paper or silicone liners. Cut the chilled dough into 2½-inch squares (use a ruler to make straight cuts and equal-size squares) and transfer them to the prepared sheet pans, setting them 1 inch apart. As you work, return the dough to the freezer as many times as necessary to keep it firm. Put each pan in the freezer one last time for a couple of minutes so that the cookies will hold their shape when baked. (If you like, you can use a knife to even out the edges of the cookies once they're cold.) Bake for 15 to 18 minutes, until the cookies have begun to brown around the edges. Let cool completely on the pans.

6. When the cookies have cooled, line three sheet pans with parchment paper. Temper the chocolate using any of the tempering techniques listed on page 126, then bring it back to working temperature. When the chocolate is ready, dip the graham crackers: drop each graham cracker into the chocolate, use a fork to make sure it's fully submerged, then scoop it out of the chocolate with two forks. Tip the cookie a bit to let excess chocolate drip back into the bowl, then scrape the fork and bottom of the cookie along the edge of the bowl to remove more excess chocolate and set it on one of the prepared pans. When all the cookies have been dipped, put the pans aside in a cool, dry place to let the chocolate set. ★

When cutting these cookies, spray the knife and the ruler with a vegetable oil spray to keep them from sticking to the dough.

When you refrigerate or freeze cookie dough, wrap it in two layers of plastic wrap to keep it from absorbing smells from other foods or developing freezer burn.

Make Ahead
The cookie dough can be refrigerated for up to 1 week or frozen for up to 1 month. Once baked and dipped, the cookies can be stored in an airtight container at room temperature for up to 2 weeks.

Whoopie Pies

Makes 14 whoopie pies

The whoopie pie is fairly simple—just two pieces of cake filled with frosting—but in the Northeast, it inspires devotion and a bit of controversy. Pennsylvanians claim that Amish mothers invented the dessert to use up leftover cake batter. But Mainers purport to have originated the treat and named it for the 1928 show tune "Makin' Whoopee!" We don't like to take sides, but our version is a Maine-style whoopie, which means that it has a filling made from our homemade marshmallow fluff. We make it with a dense, rich chocolate cake that is very similar to our Chocolate Layer Cake. Pictured on page 62.

Cakes

2 extra-large eggs

¼ cup vegetable oil

1½ teaspoons pure vanilla extract

1 cup unsweetened Dutch-process cocoa powder

3 cups all-purpose flour

½ teaspoon baking powder

2¼ teaspoons baking soda

½ teaspoon salt

½ cup (1 stick) unsalted butter, at room temperature

1½ cups granulated sugar

1½ cups whole milk

Cinnamon Filling

4 tablespoons (½ stick) unsalted butter, at room temperature

½ cup confectioners' sugar

1 teaspoon pure vanilla extract

½ cup Marshmallow Sauce (page 165)

½ teaspoon ground cinnamon

Special Tool

1½-ounce (3-tablespoon) ice cream scoop (optional, see page 19)

recipe continues on the next page

Make the Cakes

1. Preheat the oven to 350°F. Line four sheet pans with parchment paper or silicone liners. In a small bowl, mix the eggs, oil, and vanilla. Sift the cocoa powder into a medium bowl, then add the flour, baking powder, baking soda, and salt and whisk together; set both bowls aside.

2. In the bowl of a stand mixer fitted with the paddle attachment, cream the butter and granulated sugar on medium for 5 minutes, stopping the mixer halfway through to scrape down the sides and bottom of the bowl with a rubber spatula. Turn the mixer to low and slowly add the egg mixture. When the batter comes together, stop the mixer, scrape down the sides and bottom of the bowl very well to incorporate any unmixed ingredients, and then beat on high for 1 minute, until the batter is smooth and forms ribbons. Stop the mixer and scrape down the sides and bottom of the bowl.

3. Add one-third of the flour mixture and mix on low until just combined. Scrape down the sides and bottom of the bowl and add half of the milk to the batter. Mix on low until just incorporated, then scrape down the sides and bottom. Repeat with another third of the dry ingredients and the remaining milk, scraping down the bowl well after each addition, then add the remaining flour mixture, mix until just incorporated, and scrape down the bowl. Remove the bowl and finish mixing by hand, using a rubber spatula in a beating motion and scraping down the sides and bottom of the bowl to ensure all the ingredients are evenly incorporated and there are no streaks.

4. Using a 1½-ounce ice cream scoop or a ¼-cup measure, scoop out the batter into little mounds and place them at least 2 inches apart on the prepared pans. (Stagger the scoops so that they have as much room between them as possible.) You should have 6 to 8 scoops on each sheet. Use the back of the scoop to flatten the mounds just a little bit, rubbing them with a circular motion. Wet your fingers and pat in any peaks of batter that are sticking out. (If you're using a cup measure, you may also have to pat the mounds into little domes; the cakes will hold their shape as they rise and expand in the oven.) Tap the pans on the counter firmly to release any air bubbles. Bake the cakes for 12 to 15 minutes, until a paring knife inserted into the center of a cake comes out clean. (The cakes may develop little cracks in their tops.)

Make the Filling

1. In the bowl of a stand mixer fitted with the paddle attachment, cream the butter and confectioners' sugar on medium until incorporated, then turn the mixer to high and beat for 2 minutes, until the mixture is creamy and light. Add the vanilla and beat on high until incorporated, then use a rubber spatula to scrape down the sides and bottom of the bowl and beat again for a few seconds until everything is well combined.

2. Remove the bowl, add the marshmallow sauce, and use a rubber spatula to gently fold and mix everything together until combined. Add the cinnamon, and gently stir and fold until it is well distributed.

Assemble the Whoopie Pies

Transfer the cinnamon filling to a pastry bag and pipe a ½-inch-thick circle of filling onto the flat side of half of the cakes, leaving a ¼- to ½-inch space between the filling and the edge of the cake. Place the flat sides of the unfilled cakes on top of the filling to create sandwiches, and press gently so that the filling comes almost to the edge of the sandwiches. Put the whoopie pies in the refrigerator to firm up for at least 15 minutes before serving. ★

Make Ahead

The baked cakes can be wrapped in two layers of plastic wrap and kept at room temperature for 3 to 4 days or frozen for up to 1 week. The assembled whoopie pies can be kept in the refrigerator for 2 to 3 days.

Chocolate Canoes with Vanilla Cream Filling

Makes 16 canoes

This fun treat is our homage to the classic Twinkie. When Jon was growing up, he loved convenience store sweets. Every winter, he and his brothers would go out and shovel snow for their neighbors, and when they had enough money, they'd head to the store and stock up on cookies, cupcakes, Devil Dogs, and, of course, lots of Twinkies. Our version is made with a chocolate chiffon cake, rather than the traditional vanilla, but the cake, made with vegetable oil for a light, tender crumb, is airy and bouncy with a texture that reminds us of the original in all the right ways. With a little bit of vanilla cream filling in the center, it's the perfect chocolate homage to one of our favorite guilty pleasures. Pictured on page 62.

Chocolate Canoes

¼ cup unsweetened Dutch-process cocoa powder

6 tablespoons boiling water

1 teaspoon pure vanilla extract

3 extra-large egg yolks

3 tablespoons vegetable oil

¾ cup plus 2 tablespoons cake flour

¾ cup plus 3 tablespoons granulated sugar

1 teaspoon baking powder

¼ teaspoon salt

5 extra-large egg whites

½ teaspoon cream of tartar

Vegetable oil spray

Cream Filling

1 extra-large egg white

3 tablespoons confectioners' sugar

2 tablespoons water

6 tablespoons granulated sugar

7 tablespoons unsalted butter, at room temperature, cut into ½-inch cubes

½ teaspoon pure vanilla extract

Pinch of salt

Special Tools

Nonstick cream canoe pan and cream injector

tip

When you separate the eggs, make sure there are no drops of yolk in the egg whites because it will keep the whites from whipping up properly.

Make the Canoes

1. Preheat the oven to 350°F. In a small bowl, whisk the cocoa powder and boiling water together until the cocoa has dissolved, then add the vanilla. In another small bowl, whisk the egg yolks and oil together; set both bowls aside.

2. Into the bowl of a stand mixer fitted with the paddle attachment, sift together the cake flour, ¾ cup plus 2 tablespoons of the sugar, the baking powder, and salt. Add the egg yolk mixture and beat on medium speed until combined, about 30 seconds. Add the cocoa mixture and beat on medium-high until combined, then use a rubber spatula to scrape down the sides and bottom of the bowl; beat until everything is well combined, about 30 seconds. Pour the mixture into a separate bowl and set it aside. Clean the mixing bowl well and dry it thoroughly.

recipe continues on the next page

3. Put the egg whites in the clean bowl of the stand mixer. Using the whisk attachment, whip the egg whites on medium until they are very frothy and start to build volume, about 2 minutes. Add the cream of tartar and whisk on medium-high until the whites hold soft peaks, about 2 minutes. Add the remaining 1 tablespoon sugar and beat until just combined, about 30 seconds. Scrape down the sides and bottom of the bowl, then whip on medium-high until the mixture holds very stiff, shiny peaks, about 1 minute.

4. Add half of the whipped egg whites to the chocolate batter and use a rubber spatula to fold and mix the two together until combined. Add the remaining egg whites and fold them in until everything is well combined and the batter no longer has streaks.

5. Spray canoe molds with vegetable oil spray and use a spoon to fill each canoe mold halfway with the batter. Drag the tip of a paring knife through each portion of batter to release any air bubbles.

6. Bake for 15 minutes. If the canoes have domed up above the edge of the pan, spray a sheet of parchment paper with vegetable oil spray and flip the entire pan onto it to help them compress a little. Let them cool just a bit, so that they are warm but not hot, then run the tip of a small offset spatula or a butter knife between the sides of the canoes and the pan to make sure they're not sticking, and flip them out of the pan. If the canoes have formed any ridges sticking out of their sides, use a paring knife to trim them. (If your canoe pan only has eight wells, let the pan cool to room temperature before filling it with the rest of the batter.)

Make the Filling

1. In the clean bowl of the stand mixer fitted with the clean whisk attachment, whisk the egg white on medium speed for about 90 seconds, until it becomes foamy. With the mixer on medium, slowly sprinkle in 2 tablespoons of the confectioners' sugar. Stop the mixer and use a rubber spatula to scrape down the sides of the bowl. Turn the mixer back to high and whisk the egg white until it is glossy and holds very stiff peaks, 1½ to 2 minutes.

2. In a small saucepan, combine the water and granulated sugar and bring to a boil over high heat. When the mixture starts to boil, let it boil for exactly 1 minute. Turn the mixer to low and pour the sugar syrup into the egg white in a slow, steady stream, then turn the mixer to high and whip everything together until the side of the mixing bowl has cooled to room temperature, about 3 minutes.

3. Turn the mixer to low and drop the pieces of butter into the mixer one at a time, waiting 10 seconds between each piece. Turn the mixer to high and whisk for 30 seconds. Add the remaining 1 tablespoon confectioners' sugar, the vanilla, and salt and whisk on high for 30 seconds to incorporate.

Fill the Canoes

Put the cream filling into a cream injector and fill the canoes one at a time, adding more cream to the injector as necessary: Insert the needle into the end of the canoe—it should reach halfway through the canoe. Gently press the injector's plunger while slowly removing the needle from the canoe. Repeat on the other end of the canoe so that the cream filling extends all the way through the length of the canoe. ★

Make Ahead

The unfilled chocolate canoes can be wrapped individually in plastic wrap and frozen for up to 2 weeks. The filling can be refrigerated for up to 10 days or frozen for up to 1 month. The filled canoes can be kept in the refrigerator for 2 to 3 days.

Above and Beyond
Orange Cream Filling

For a twist on the recipe above, add the zest of 1 orange to the cream filling when you add the vanilla extract. ★

Contruction Instructions

Brownie Sundae

Makes 1 Sundae

6

Use the back of a small spoon to make an indentation on the top of the whipped cream and place **1 fresh, candied, or brandied cherry** in it.

5

Top the sundae with a scattering of **chocolate shavings** (see "How to Plate like The Chocolate Room," page 150).

4

With a large spoon, place a dollop of **Vanilla Whipped Cream** (page 160) on top of the ice cream.

2

Make a very generous scoop of **Vanilla Ice Cream** (page 157) or any of the other ice creams we make at The Chocolate Room (see "Drinks and Accompaniments"), about the size of a tennis ball, and nestle it on top of the brownie.

3

Use a ladle to pour about 4 tablespoons **heated Hot Fudge** (page 161) around the ice cream onto the brownie, so that it makes a small pool for the ice cream.

1

Place **1 Brownie** (page 69) in the bottom of a wide ice cream serving bowl or coupe and heat it in the microwave for 20 seconds, until it is just warmed through.

Banana Cream Pie
recipe on page 99

pies

How to Bake the Perfect Chocolate Pie Crust

Baking pie crusts doesn't have to be hard; in fact, if you're using our very forgiving (and delicious) Chocolate Pie Crust (page 92), it could be some of the easiest baking you've ever done. When we make pies, we often whip up dozens of pie crusts all at once. Over the years, we've developed a few tricks that make baking consistent, perfectly baked pie crusts a snap.

The Perfect Rolling Pin

When we roll out the dough for pie crusts (or for our Chocolate Sandwich Cookies, page 75), we use a baker's rolling pin that is essentially just a 20-inch-long, 2-inch-thick dowel. It doesn't have handles or tapered ends, and it's longer than the dough will be when it's rolled flat, so it helps us apply even, uniform pressure across the whole surface of the dough at all times.

Always Rolling Away

To roll out the dough, place the rolling pin in the center of the disk of dough and push it away from you, then turn the dough a few degrees and repeat the motion. If you're always pushing the rolling pin away from you, rather than pushing it at an angle or pulling it toward yourself, you'll exert consistent pressure with each pass and it will be easier to roll the dough into a flat, even round.

Check the Edges

When rolling out pie dough, it's always best to place it between two sheets of parchment paper to keep it from sticking, but this can keep you from being able to tell how thick the dough is. When the dough is close to being ¼ to ½ inch thick, lift the sides of the parchment on top of the dough and check the edges to make sure they look like they're the same thickness. If one side looks thicker than the others, you can even it out as you finish rolling the dough. (Because our pie dough is very malleable, you can also check for evenness by running the palm of your hand along the finished dough and literally pushing it flat if you feel any thick ridges.)

Baking Pie Crusts in Aluminum Tins

Our pies can be made in any kind of ceramic or metal pie plates, but we usually use two disposable aluminum tins—one to hold the crust and one to keep the crust in place instead of parchment paper and pie weights. Here's how:

1

Preheat the oven to 350°F.

2

Roll the dough out to ¼ to ½ inch thick and transfer it to a disposable aluminum pie tin, tucking it into place so that it is flush against the tin.

3

Place a second disposable aluminum pie tin on top of the dough. Press the tin down slightly to help the dough take the shape of the tins.

4

Use a paring knife to trim off any dough that sticks out beyond the tins' edges.

5

Place the pie tins upside down on a sheet pan. (Baking the crust upside down will keep it from shrinking while it bakes.)

6

Bake the crust for 45 minutes. Let it cool on the pan, then flip it right-side up, remove the top tin, and fill the crust with the desired filling.

Above and Beyond
Pie Crust Crumbs

After the crust has been rolled out and cut, lay the leftover scraps of dough flat on a parchment paper–lined sheet pan. Bake for 15 minutes, then let cool to room temperature. Break the crust up with your hands, transfer to a food processor, and pulse into fine crumbs.

Above and Beyond
Pie Crust Cookies

Knead any unused dough briefly with 1 to 2 tablespoons chopped nuts or dried fruit, roll the dough into a log, and refrigerate until firm, at least 2 hours. Preheat the oven to 350°F. Use a chef's knife to slice the log of dough crosswise into ¼-inch-thick cookies. Bake on a parchment paper–lined sheet pan for 20 minutes. The cookies will hold their shape as they bake and will be crisp and dry when cooled.

Chocolate Pie Crust

This simple, cookielike crust is technically a tart crust, rather than a flaky pie crust leavened by butter, but it's so flavorful and easy to work with that we use it for almost all our pies. This recipe makes a 9- to 10-inch pie crust. If you're making a smaller pie and have lots of dough left over, you can use it to make some Pie Crust Cookies (see page 91). The baking instructions here are written for traditional metal or ceramic pie tins, but for a few tricks for rolling out the dough and baking crusts in disposable aluminum pie tins, like we do in the cafés, see "How to Bake the Perfect Chocolate Pie Crust" (page 90).

2¼ cups all-purpose flour

½ cup unsweetened Dutch-process cocoa powder

¼ teaspoon salt

1 cup (2 sticks) unsalted butter,
at room temperature

1¼ cups confectioners' sugar, sifted

1 extra-large egg

1 extra-large egg yolk

1. In a small bowl, mix together the flour, cocoa powder, and salt; set aside. In the bowl of a stand mixer fitted with the paddle attachment, beat the butter and confectioners' sugar together on medium-low until very creamy and fluffy, about 3 minutes. Add the egg and egg yolk and beat on low until incorporated, then use a rubber spatula to scrape down the sides and bottom of the bowl and beat for a few seconds until everything is well combined.

2. Add the flour mixture and mix on low until incorporated. Remove the bowl from the mixer and finish mixing by hand, using a rubber spatula and scraping down the sides and bottom of the bowl to ensure that all the ingredients are evenly incorporated.

3. Form the dough into a disk and wrap it in two layers of plastic wrap. Refrigerate the dough for at least 4 hours, preferably overnight.

4. When the dough has chilled, remove it from the refrigerator and let it warm up until it is just a little cooler than room temperature.

Roll Out and Bake the Crust

1. Preheat the oven to 350°F. Place the dough disk between two sheets of parchment paper and roll it out until it is ¼ inch thick. Transfer the dough to a pie pan and press it into place, then trim off the excess dough so the edge is flush with the edge of the pan. (The dough is very malleable, so if it rips when you transfer it, simply patch it back together.) Place the pan in the freezer for 10 minutes.

2. Prick the chilled dough all over with a fork, line it with parchment paper, and fill the parchment with pie weights or dried beans. Bake the crust for 15 to 20 minutes, until the edges are set, then remove the pie weights and the parchment and bake until the crust is set on the bottom, about 5 minutes. Let the crust cool completely before filling it. ★

Make Ahead

The dough can be refrigerated for up to 2 weeks or frozen for up to 1 month. The baked crust can be wrapped in two layers of plastic wrap and kept at room temperature for up to 1 week.

Chocolate Cream Pie

Makes one 9-inch pie

Chocolate cream pies first started appearing in American recipe books toward the end of the nineteenth century. The original recipes would look surprisingly familiar to anyone who has made chocolate cream pie before; they call for making a custard out of chocolate, eggs, sugar, and cornstarch mixed with water or milk and pouring it into a pie shell. Given how tastes have changed in the past century, it's a little surprising how well this recipe has stood the test of time, but the brilliance of this pie lies in its simplicity—each bite is luscious and creamy and comforting. Pictured on page 97.

4 ounces dark chocolate (preferably 70% cacao), coarsely chopped

2 extra-large egg yolks

2 tablespoons cornstarch

2 tablespoons plus ⅓ cup granulated sugar

1 cup whole milk

½ teaspoon pure vanilla extract

1 cup heavy cream

1 tablespoon confectioners' sugar

½ cup Chocolate Syrup (page 162), plus extra for drizzling

1 (9-inch) Chocolate Pie Crust (page 92), baked and cooled

3 cups Vanilla Whipped Cream (page 160), whipped to very stiff peaks

1. Melt the chocolate in the top of a double boiler, stirring to keep it from burning, or microwave it in 20-second intervals, stirring after each interval, until it becomes liquid. In a medium bowl, whisk together the egg yolks, cornstarch, and 2 tablespoons of the granulated sugar; set aside. In a small saucepan, combine the milk, remaining ⅓ cup granulated sugar, and the vanilla and heat over medium-high heat, whisking occasionally, until the milk starts to steam.

2. Add a couple tablespoons of the hot milk to the eggs and whisk to incorporate so that the egg mixture becomes fluid, then, while whisking continuously, add the rest of the milk mixture in a slow, steady stream to temper the eggs.

3. Pour the mixture back into the saucepan and cook over medium-high heat, whisking continuously, until the pastry cream thickens and has large bubbles. Remove the saucepan from the heat, add the melted chocolate, and whisk until the pastry

cream is homogenous and no visible streaks remain. Strain the pastry cream through a fine-mesh sieve into a shallow pan, pressing it through with a rubber spatula. Spread it out in a thin layer and press plastic wrap directly against the surface of the pastry cream to prevent a skin from forming. Refrigerate the pastry cream until very cold, at least 2 hours.

4. Once the pastry cream has chilled, in the bowl of a stand mixer fitted with the whisk attachment, whip the heavy cream on medium, adding the confectioners' sugar a little at a time, until it holds very stiff peaks. Remove the bowl, add the chilled pastry cream, and mix and fold with a rubber spatula until thoroughly combined.

recipe continues on the next page

Assemble the Pie

1. Pour the chocolate syrup into the pie crust and use a small offset spatula or the back of a spoon to smooth it into a thin, uniform layer. Put the crust in the freezer for 10 minutes to firm up the syrup. Pour the chocolate cream filling over the chocolate sauce and use a small offset spatula or rubber spatula to smooth it out to fill the crust. Refrigerate the pie for at least 4 hours to firm up the filling.

2. Spread one-third of the Vanilla Whipped Cream onto the top of the pie and use a small offset spatula or rubber spatula to smooth it across the pie in a uniform layer. Transfer the remaining whipped cream to a pastry bag fitted with a large closed star tip, and pipe large rosettes all over the top of the pie, completely covering the surface. (See "Using a Pastry Bag," page 108, for directions for making rosettes.) Drizzle a zigzag of chocolate syrup over the whipped cream before serving.

Make Ahead

The chocolate pastry cream can be refrigerated for up to 4 days. The finished pie can be refrigerated for 3 to 4 days. ★

Chocolate Pecan Pie

Makes one 10-inch pie

There's something decadent about adding a little bit of chocolate to a classic like pecan pie. The long-loved flavors are still there, but they're amplified just a little bit by the richness of the chocolate. We make this pie with a regular pie crust instead of our usual chocolate crust; we think the classic flavor and flaky texture adds a nice traditional touch. If you're particularly partial to the crisp, candylike surface that forms on top of the pie, you can use this same recipe to make an 11-inch tart, which will give you a wider surface area. Pictured on page 96.

Crust

1¼ cups all-purpose flour, plus extra for dusting

½ teaspoon salt

½ teaspoon granulated sugar

½ cup (1 stick) unsalted butter, cold, cut into small pieces

¼ cup ice water

Filling

2½ ounces dark chocolate (preferably 60% cacao), coarsely chopped

3 tablespoons unsalted butter

½ cup granulated sugar

¾ cup light corn syrup

2 extra-large eggs

1 teaspoon pure vanilla extract

¼ teaspoon salt

1½ cups pecan halves

 tip

The key to flaky pie crust is to keep the butter very cold. After you've cut the butter into little pieces, it is best to leave it in the refrigerator until just before you use it.

Make the Crust

1. In a food processor, combine the flour, salt, sugar, and butter and process for about 10 seconds, until the mixture resembles coarse meal. Drizzle in the ice water 1 tablespoon at a time, pulsing the processor a couple of times after each addition. Stop when most of the dough comes together into a single clump. Turn the dough out onto a clean work surface and knead it two or three times so that it all comes together. Shape it into a flat disk, wrap it in plastic wrap, and refrigerate for at least 1 hour.

2. On a lightly floured surface, roll out the dough into a 12-inch circle. Fit the circle of dough into a 10-inch pie pan and tuck the overhanging dough under to fit snugly along the top edge of the pie pan. Pinch the edge of the crust to create a wavy pattern. Cover the crust with plastic wrap and refrigerate for 20 minutes.

Make the Filling

1. Melt the chocolate and butter together in the top of a double boiler, stirring to keep the chocolate from burning, or microwave them together in 30-second intervals, stirring after each interval, until they become liquid. Whisk the butter and chocolate briskly until combined, then set aside to cool a little.

2. In a small saucepan, heat the sugar and corn syrup over medium heat, stirring to dissolve the sugar. Bring the syrup to a boil, then immediately remove from the heat to keep the mixture from bubbling over. Set the syrup aside to cool a little.

3. Put the eggs in a large bowl and beat with a whisk until smooth. Add the chocolate mixture and whisk to combine; while whisking, drizzle in the sugar syrup, then add the vanilla and salt. Fold in the pecan halves with a wooden spoon.

Assemble and Bake the Pie

Preheat the oven to 350°F. Pour the filling into the chilled pie shell. (It will not fill the pie shell.) Place the pie plate on a sheet pan to catch any filling that bubbles over. Bake the pie for 1 hour, until the crust is golden, the filling doesn't wobble much when you shake the pan, and the edges of the filling have a bubbling, crisp texture. Allow the pie to cool thoroughly before serving. ★

Make Ahead

The raw pie crust can be frozen for up to 1 month. The filling, without the nuts in it, will keep in the refrigerator for up to 1 week. The baked pie can be refrigerated for 3 to 4 days.

Serving Suggestion

Vanilla Ice Cream (page 157)

Chocolate Cream Pie
recipe on page 93

Frozen White Chocolate Key Lime Pie
recipe on page 100

Banana Cream Pie

Makes one 9-inch pie

Bananas took the United States by storm in the 1880s and early 1900s, when ads capitalized on the fruit's healthful properties with slogans like, "Bananas Give Children Energy and Strength." Soon there were banana syrups, banana remedies to cure colds and fevers, a banana-based "coffee substitute," and popular songs about the fruit, like 1922's "Yes! We Have No Bananas."

The first banana cream pies called for sliced bananas accompanied by a separate layer of pudding, and that's exactly how we make our version. Our chocolaty spin on this classic dessert was Naomi's brainchild—instead of just combining the bananas with a chocolate pudding, we make a classic vanilla cream and then add a layer of chocolate ganache around the sliced bananas. We also caramelize the bananas slightly to bring out their flavor so they'll stand up to the rich, dark flavor of the semisweet ganache.

2 extra-large egg yolks

2 tablespoons cornstarch

2 tablespoons plus ⅓ cup granulated sugar

1 cup whole milk

½ teaspoon pure vanilla extract

¾ cup heavy cream

1½ tablespoons light corn syrup

9 ounces dark chocolate (preferably 60% cacao), coarsely chopped

½ cup (1 stick) unsalted butter

1 cup dark brown sugar

½ teaspoon ground cinnamon

½ cup dark rum

4 or 5 ripe bananas (depending on size), cut crosswise into ¼- to ⅓-inch rounds

1 (9-inch) Chocolate Pie Crust (page 92), baked and cooled

3 cups Vanilla Whipped Cream (page 160), whipped to very stiff peaks

Chocolate shavings (see "How to Plate Desserts like The Chocolate Room," page 150)

1. In a medium bowl, whisk together the egg yolks, cornstarch, and 2 tablespoons of the granulated sugar; set aside. In a small saucepan, combine the milk, the remaining ⅓ cup granulated sugar, and the vanilla and heat over medium-high heat, whisking occasionally, until the milk starts to steam.

2. Add a couple tablespoons of the hot milk to the eggs and whisk to incorporate so that the egg mixture becomes fluid, then, while whisking continuously, add the rest of the milk mixture in a slow, steady stream to temper the eggs.

3. Pour the mixture back into the saucepan and cook over medium-high heat, whisking continuously, until the pastry cream thickens and has large bubbles. Strain the pastry cream through a fine-mesh sieve into a shallow pan,

pressing it through with a rubber spatula. Spread it out in a thin layer and press plastic wrap directly against the surface of the pastry cream to prevent a skin from forming. Refrigerate the pastry cream until very cold, at least 2 hours.

4. In a medium saucepan, combine the heavy cream and the corn syrup and bring to a boil over medium-high heat, stirring occasionally to keep the corn syrup from sticking to the bottom of the pan. Remove from the heat and add the chocolate. Set aside until the chocolate melts, about 5 minutes. Whisk until the ganache is smooth and homogenous, then set aside to cool until it is still fluid and but only slightly warm.

recipe continues on the next page

5. In a large pot, cook the butter and brown sugar over medium heat, stirring occasionally, until both have melted and the mixture comes to a boil. Add the cinnamon and rum (the mixture will bubble up when you add the rum) and whisk to combine. Gently add the bananas and cook, stirring occasionally, for 5 minutes, until the bananas are soft but not falling apart. Remove the bananas with a slotted spoon, draining away as much of the cooking liquid as possible, and set aside in a small bowl to cool to room temperature.

6. Spread the chilled pastry cream over the bottom of the pie crust, using a rubber spatula or small off-set spatula to make a smooth, even layer. Spoon the cooked bananas on top of the pastry cream, discarding any extra syrup, and spread them out. Top the bananas with the chocolate ganache and tap the pan firmly on the counter so the ganache can get between the pieces of banana. Refrigerate the pie until the ganache is firm, about 30 minutes.

7. Put one-third of the whipped cream on top of the pie and use a small offset spatula or rubber spatula to smooth it into a uniform layer. Transfer the remaining whipped cream to a pastry bag fitted with a large closed star tip and pipe large rosettes all over the top of the pie, completely covering the surface. (See "Using a Pastry Bag," page 108, for directions for making rosettes.) Chill the pie for a few minutes and top it with chocolate shavings before serving. ★

Make Ahead

The pastry cream can be refrigerated for up to 4 days. The chocolate ganache can be refrigerated for up to 1 week. The cooked bananas can be refrigerated for 3 to 4 days. The assembled pie can be refrigerated for 2 to 3 days.

Frozen White Chocolate Key Lime Pie

Makes one 9-inch Pie

Tiny, pungent Florida Key limes are a perfect fruit to pair with white chocolate. The bright, tart flavor of the limes is a fantastic foil for the chocolate's silky sweetness. Traditional Key lime pies mix the fruit's juice with sweetened condensed milk and egg yolks to make a custard. For our chocolaty version of this dessert, we add fluffy egg whites and whipped cream—and then we turn the whole thing into a frozen treat. If you can't find Key limes in the market, you can make this recipe with a combination of bottled Key lime juice and regular lime zest, or you can use this recipe to make a pie with oranges, grapefruit, or any other kind of citrus. (As with all our recipes that use uncooked egg, we use pasteurized eggs when we make this mousse in our cafés.) Pictured on page 97.

1 (9-inch) Chocolate Pie Crust (page 92), baked and cooled

6 Key limes or 1½ tablespoons Key lime juice and 3 regular limes

1½ ounces white chocolate, roughly chopped

2 extra-large eggs

1 cup heavy cream

4 tablespoons granulated sugar

1. Zest the limes on a microplane zester or on the smallest holes on a box grater, and put the zest in a small bowl. If using fresh Key limes, juice the limes. Mix 1½ tablespoons lime juice into the zest and set the bowl aside. (Discard the remaining juice or set it aside for another use.) Melt the white chocolate in the top of a double boiler, stirring to keep the chocolate from burning, or microwave it in 15-second intervals, stirring after each interval, until it becomes liquid; set aside. Separate the egg yolks and whites and set them both aside.

2. In a stand mixer with a whisk attachment, whip the cream on medium until it holds soft peaks, about 3 minutes. Scrape the bottom of the bowl with a rubber spatula to mix in any liquid that hasn't been worked into the whipped cream and whip the cream again for a few seconds until the liquid has also formed soft peaks. Transfer the whipped cream to a small bowl and put it in the refrigerator to chill. Clean the mixer and dry thoroughly.

3. Put the egg yolks and 1 tablespoon of the sugar in the mixer fitted with the whisk attachment and whip them on high until they have become pale and ribbony, about 4 minutes. Use a rubber spatula to scrape the sides and bottom of the mixing bowl and then whisk again for a few seconds until everything is well combined. Transfer the whipped yolks to a large mixing bowl. Add the melted chocolate to the egg yolks and use a rubber spatula to fold the ingredients together until they are well combined. Add the lime juice and zest to the egg and chocolate mixture and fold everything together until thoroughly combined. Clean the mixer and dry thoroughly.

4. Put the egg whites and remaining 3 tablespoons sugar in the mixer fitted with the whisk attachment and whip them on medium-high until the whites form very stiff peaks, about 3 minutes. Add half of the whites to the chocolate-lime mixture, and use a rubber spatula to gently fold and mix the two together until they are thoroughly combined, then repeat with the remaining egg whites. Remove the whipped cream from the refrigerator, add it to the egg mixture, and fold everything together until the mixture is uniform.

5. Pour the filling into the baked pie crust and cover the pie with plastic wrap. Freeze the entire pie for at least 1 hour. To serve, remove the pie from the freezer and allow it to soften for just a couple of minutes before slicing; return any unused portion of the pie to the freezer immediately. ★

Because this pie is served frozen, it is important to make sure that you have a very thin pie crust, otherwise it will be very difficult to cut through. For the best results when cutting the pie, heat a chef's knife by running it under very hot water and then wiping it dry. Repeat for every slice of pie to keep the knife hot.

Make Ahead
The finished pie can be frozen for up to 4 days.

Boston Cream Pie

Makes one 9-inch "pie"

This classic dessert is not really a pie. As anyone from Massachusetts can tell you, it's actually two layers of vanilla cake with vanilla pastry cream between them and chocolate frosting on top. This "pie" is a descendant of American jelly cakes (layers of cake with jelly between them) that were served in wedge slices. By the 1860s, some cooks were substituting pastry cream for the jelly, but it wasn't until the 1950s, when the chocolate frosting was added to the equation, that the dessert became an American icon. The Boston cream pie was served at the "American Exhibition" that introduced the Soviet Union to American consumer goods in 1959; it was a favorite in the Kennedy White House; and Frank Sinatra requested it for his birthday.

Our version of this dessert is filled with Bavarian cream, which is creamier and lighter than straight pastry cream, and is topped with our rich chocolate frosting. We bake the cake portion in a pie tin, but you could also bake it in a 9-inch cake pan and cut the corners off to make the classic dome shape.

Vanilla Cake

3 extra-large eggs

1 teaspoon pure vanilla extract

1¼ cups cake flour

3½ teaspoons baking powder

Pinch of salt

6 tablespoons (¾ stick) unsalted butter, at room temperature, plus extra for greasing the pan

1¼ cups granulated sugar

½ cup sour cream

½ cup whole milk

Cream Filling

1 extra-large egg

1 extra-large egg yolk

2 tablespoons cornstarch

5 tablespoons granulated sugar

1 cup whole milk

½ teaspoon pure vanilla extract

¾ cup heavy cream

2 teaspoons confectioners' sugar

To Assemble

½ cup granulated sugar

½ cup water

½ recipe Chocolate Frosting (page 31)

tip

The material the pie plate is made of will affect how long the batter bakes: a metal pie tin will heat faster (and conduct heat more efficiently) than a ceramic or Pyrex pie plate. When we make this "pie" in the café, we use disposable aluminum pie tins. The aluminum lets the cake bake faster than traditional pie plates, and because it is bendable, it's easier to remove the cake from the tin.

recipe continues on the next page

Make the Cake

1. Preheat the oven to 350°F. Cut a circle of parchment paper to fit the bottom of a 9-inch pie plate. Lightly butter the pie plate, line it with the parchment circle, and butter the parchment. Line 6 wells of a standard muffin tin with paper liners.

2. In a small bowl, beat the eggs lightly with the vanilla until they are broken up. In a large bowl, sift together the cake flour, baking powder, and salt. Set both bowls aside.

3. In the bowl of a stand mixer fitted with the paddle attachment, cream the butter and sugar on medium for 1 minute. Stop the mixer, scrape down the sides and bottom of the bowl, and beat on medium for 2 minutes, until the mixture is very light and fluffy. Add the egg mixture and mix on medium-low until the mixture just comes together, about 20 seconds. Scrape down the sides and bottom of the bowl, then mix on medium until there are no lumps or unmixed ingredients, about 15 seconds.

4. Add one-third of the flour mixture to the batter and mix on low until just combined. Scrape down the sides and bottom of the bowl and add half of the sour cream. Mix on low until just incorporated, about 30 seconds, then scrape down the sides and bottom of the bowl. Repeat with another third of the flour mixture and the remaining sour cream, scraping down the bowl well after each addition. Add the remaining flour mixture, mix until just incorporated, and scrape down the bowl.

5. With the mixer on low, add the milk in a thin stream, then mix until the batter is uniform, about 20 seconds. Remove the bowl from the mixer and finish mixing by hand, using a rubber spatula in a beating motion and scraping the sides and bottom of the bowl to ensure that all the ingredients are evenly incorporated and the batter is completely smooth and lump-free.

6. Fill the lined muffin cups with about ¼ cup of batter each. Pour the rest of the batter into the pie plate. Bake the cupcakes for 20 minutes; bake the cake in the pie plate for 20 to 30 minutes.

When finished, the cake should spring back lightly when pressed with your fingers and a paring knife inserted into the center of the cake and cupcakes should come out clean. Let the cake and cupcakes cool in the pans to room temperature. Reduce the oven temperature to 300°F.

7. Run a paring knife between the cake and the sides of the tin and turn it out onto a cutting board; the part of the cake that was in the bottom of the pie tin will be the top of the dome-shaped "pie." Trim off any bits of cake that stuck out over the edge of the pie tin so there are no "feet" at the bottom of the dome, then cut it in half horizontally to make two layers. (For the easiest way to get even layers, see "How to Assemble and Frost a Perfect, Showstopping Cake," page 24.)

8. Break each cupcake into 6 to 8 pieces, put them on a sheet pan, and bake for 25 minutes to dry them out. Let cool to room temperature, then transfer to a food processor and grind into fine crumbs.

Make the Filling

1. In a medium bowl, whisk together the egg, egg yolk, cornstarch, and granulated sugar until combined; set aside. In a small saucepan, combine the milk and vanilla and heat over medium-high heat, whisking occasionally, until the milk starts to steam.

2. Add a couple tablespoons of the hot milk to the eggs and whisk to incorporate so that the egg mixture becomes fluid, then, while whisking continuously, add the rest of the milk mixture in a slow, steady stream to temper the eggs.

3. Pour the mixture back into the saucepan and cook over medium-high heat, whisking continuously, until the pastry cream thickens and has large bubbles. Strain the pastry cream through a fine-mesh sieve into a shallow pan, pressing it through with a rubber spatula. Spread it out in a thin layer and press plastic wrap directly against the surface of the pastry cream to prevent a skin from forming. Refrigerate the pastry cream until it is very cold, at least 2 hours. Clean the mixer bowl and dry it thoroughly.

4. In the clean bowl of the stand mixer fitted with the whisk attachment, whip the heavy cream on medium, adding the confectioners' sugar a little at a time, until it holds very stiff peaks. Remove the bowl, add the chilled pastry cream, and mix and fold together with a rubber spatula until thoroughly combined.

Assemble the "Pie"

1. Combine the granulated sugar and the water in a small saucepan and heat over medium heat, stirring occasionally, until the sugar has dissolved; set the simple syrup aside to cool to room temperature.

2. Put a dab of the cream filling on a serving plate to hold the cake in place, then place the bottom (larger) layer of cake on the plate, cut-side up. Brush the cut sides of both layers of the cake with 2 to 3 tablespoons of simple syrup each. Cover the bottom layer with about 2 cups of the cream filling and use a rubber spatula to spread it into a thick, even layer. Top the filling with the second layer of cake, cut-side down, and refrigerate the "pie" for 30 minutes to help it firm up.

3. Spread a thick layer of the chocolate frosting on top of the cake, but leave the sides bare. Spread the remaining cream filling along the sides of the "pie," then use your hands to pat the cake crumbs onto the sides, all the way up to the top of the cake, covering all of the white pastry cream and the edges of the chocolate frosting.

4. Use the tip of a butter knife or small offset spatula to make stripes in the chocolate frosting. Refrigerate the pie for at least 1 hour before serving to firm up the filling and frosting. Serve cold. ⋆

Make Ahead

The vanilla cake can be can wrapped in two layers of plastic wrap and refrigerated for up to 5 days or frozen for up to 1 month. The pastry cream for the cream filling can be refrigerated for up to 4 days. The assembled "pie" can be kept in the refrigerator for 3 to 4 days.

Sticky Date Pudding with Chocolate Toffee Sauce
recipe on page 118

puddings
& custards

Using a Pastry Bag

At The Chocolate Room we love pastry bags. We use them for everything from decorating cakes to filling sandwich cookies to portioning out batter. All our chefs have developed their own tricks for making pastry bags even more versatile and easier to use. Here are some of our favorite tips and tricks.

When to Use a Pastry Bag

At The Chocolate Room, we use pastry bags to do all sorts of things, but they're especially great for helping with the following tasks:

• Distributing frosting evenly around the sides of our Chocolate Layer Cake (page 27; see "How to Assemble and Frost a Perfect, Showstopping Cake," page 24)

• Piping buttercream onto our Chocolate Sandwich Cookies (page 75) so that we always have nice, even layers

• Piping the marshmallow base onto our S'mores (page 146) so the marshmallow doesn't stick to our utensils or our hands

• Portioning out batter for small cakes or custard for individual puddings

How to Fill a Pastry Bag

Here's our easy, mess-free process for filling pastry bags:

If you're using a pastry tip, place it into the point of the bag and make sure that only ¼ to ⅓ inch of the tip sticks out of the bag. Twist the bag shut behind the tip so that it stays closed while you fill the bag.

Place the point of the pastry bag in the bottom of a tall, wide-mouthed container (like the kind used for takeout soup). Open the pastry bag so that it lines the inside of the container, then fold the rest of the bag over the outside of the container.

Fill only the half of the pastry bag that's in the container—this will keep the back half of the pastry bag clean so it is easier to work with and will keep frosting or other filling from spilling out of the back of the bag.

Take the pastry bag out of the container and twist the bag closed behind the frosting or batter.

Repeat this process to refill the bag if you need to use more frosting or batter.

The Best Ways to Handle a Pastry Bag for Maximum Control

Once the pastry bag has been filled, it's important to hold it and work with it in a way that gives you control over how quickly or slowly your frosting or batter comes out of the bag. Here's how we do it:

For a firm mixture like frosting, untwist the tip of the pastry bag and push the frosting down toward the tip so there isn't any air in the tip of the bag.

Press a little bit of the frosting out of the bag onto a paper towel to see how slowly or quickly it will flow. If you're beading a cake or making rosettes (see below), practice a couple of them on a paper towel.

Always exert even, steady pressure on the pastry bag so the frosting comes out slowly and evenly.

If you overfilled the pastry bag and find that it has become unwieldy, twist the bag in the middle to cut the frosting or filling into two parts—this will give you more control over how fast it comes out of the bag.

To portion out something more liquid, like batter for small cakes or custard bases for puddings, use a pastry bag without a decorative tip and pinch the tip of the bag closed with your fingers whenever you need to stop the flow of batter.

Decorating with a Pastry Bag

In culinary school, our chefs learned to use pastry bags to make all kinds of decorations and designs, but at The Chocolate Room, there are two simple designs that we use again and again.

Frosting Beads on the Bottom of a Cake:

Gently press the pastry bag to let a small ball or "bead" of frosting out onto the bottom edge of the cake where it meets the serving plate or cake board.

When the bead is done, stop pressing on the pastry bag and gently move the tip of the bag about ¼ inch to the right of the bead—this will make a small tail so that the bead looks like a sideways raindrop.

Make the next bead on top of the raindrop tail so it covers the tail. Repeat this process until you have beads of frosting circling the entire bottom of the cake.

When you finish making the last bead on the cake, don't pull the pastry bag to the side to make a tail; instead, swirl the tip of the bag on top of the bead to make a small spiral.

Whipped Cream Rosettes:

Place a large closed star tip in your pastry bag (see "How to Fill a Pastry Bag" for proper placement) and fill the bag with whipped cream.

Gently press the pastry bag and use one continuous motion to make a large circle of whipped cream, then keep going to make a smaller circle on top of the large one.

When the rosette is done, stop pressing on the bag and lift the tip straight up, away from the rosette.

Chocolate Pudding

Makes 6 puddings

This pudding is the stuff of childhood dreams. Creamy and rich, with a mix of the comforting flavor of cocoa and the rich bite of semisweet chocolate, it's what we wish our after-school snacks had been like. This pudding is kind of an overlooked gem on our menu—many of our customers simply pass over it while looking for showier items like cakes and sundaes—but once people try it, it becomes one of the dishes they return to again and again.

5 ounces dark chocolate (preferably 60% cacao), coarsely chopped

2 tablespoons unsalted butter

2½ cups whole milk

6 tablespoons granulated sugar

1 extra-large egg

2 extra-large egg yolks

¼ teaspoon salt

2 tablespoons cornstarch

1 tablespoon unsweetened Dutch-process cocoa powder

1 teaspoon pure vanilla extract

If you don't want to use a food processor for this recipe, you can also make the pudding by simply whisking the ingredients together in a large bowl; just be sure to whisk quickly while pouring the hot liquid into the eggs so they are properly tempered.

Putting plastic wrap on the puddings while they're still hot captures the steam the puddings emit as they cool; this keeps them moist and prevents them from developing hard, rubbery surfaces.

1. Melt the chocolate and butter together in the top of a double boiler, stirring to keep the chocolate from burning, or microwave them together in 30-second intervals, stirring after each interval, until they become liquid. Whisk together briskly until combined.

2. In a medium saucepan, combine 2 cups of the milk and 3 tablespoons of the sugar and cook over medium-high heat until the milk begins to steam.

3. Meanwhile, in a food processor, combine the remaining 3 tablespoons sugar, the egg, egg yolks, salt, cornstarch, and cocoa powder and process until combined, about 20 seconds. With the food processor running, pour in about ½ cup of the hot milk in a slow, steady stream to temper the eggs.

4. Pour the mixture from the food processor into the saucepan with the remaining milk and cook over medium-high heat, whisking continuously, until the mixture starts to bubble and thicken. Remove from the heat and add the remaining ½ cup milk, then the vanilla, and finally the butter-chocolate mixture, whisking until the pudding is smooth and free of lumps.

5. While the pudding is still hot, divide it evenly among six pudding cups or small bowls. Cover each cup tightly with plastic wrap and refrigerate until the pudding is cold, at least 2 hours. ★

Make Ahead
The puddings will keep in the refrigerator, covered with plastic, for 4 to 5 days.

Serving Suggestion
Vanilla Whipped Cream (page 160) and chocolate shavings (see page 150)

Black-Bottom Butterscotch Custard

Makes 8 custards

Sometimes instead of making a dessert that is just chock-full of chocolate, we like to use our favorite ingredient sparingly, as an accompaniment to other rich flavors. This butterscotch custard is a perfect example. The custard itself is flavored with rich, sweet butterscotch, augmented by a thin layer of chocolate syrup at the bottom of each cup. The touch of bitterness from the cocoa offsets the sweetness of the butterscotch perfectly. This dessert has been on our menu for years now, and it's still a huge hit. A few months ago we even had a devoted customer stop us on the street to tell us the dessert was "life-changing." We feel the same way.

1¾ cups heavy cream

2 tablespoons pure vanilla extract

1 cup whole milk

6 extra-large egg yolks

3 tablespoons unsalted butter

¾ cup dark brown sugar

½ teaspoon salt

8 tablespoons Chocolate Syrup (page 162)

Special Tools

Eight 4-ounce (½-cup) ceramic ramekins (3¾ inches in diameter) (see page 17)

1. Combine ¾ cup of the cream and the vanilla and heat the mixture in the microwave or on the stove until steaming; cover to keep warm and set aside. Combine the remaining 1 cup cream, the milk, and the egg yolks in a separate bowl and whisk to combine; set aside.

2. In a medium saucepan, melt the butter over medium-high heat. When it begins to bubble, add the brown sugar and salt and cook, stirring continuously with a rubber spatula. (The sugar will smoke a little bit and begin to caramelize as it melts.) When the sugar has melted and the caramel has just begun to bubble, turn off the heat and add the cream-and-vanilla mixture in a slow stream, whisking continuously and standing back from the pan to avoid the steam that will erupt from the addition of the cream to the hot sugar. Once the caramel has settled down, add the milk-and-egg mixture in a slow, steady stream, whisking until well combined. Strain the mixture

through a fine-mesh sieve into a bowl and set aside to cool. When the mixture has cooled, cover it with plastic wrap and refrigerate for at least 4 hours, preferably overnight.

....

If the cream cools too much before you add it to the caramel and the sugar seizes up, cook the mixture over low heat until it is fluid again.

....

3. Once the custard base has chilled, remove it from the refrigerator and let it sit until it is almost room temperature but is still a little bit cool to the touch, about 2 hours.

recipe continues on the next page

4. Heat the chocolate syrup in the microwave or by putting the container into a pot of hot water until it is fluid. Put just enough of the chocolate syrup in the bottom of each of eight 4-ounce (½-cup) ceramic ramekins (3¾ inches in diameter) to coat—about 1 scant tablespoon—and swirl the ramekin to coat the bottom evenly. (If any of the syrup gets on the sides of the ramekin, use a paper towel to wipe it off so it doesn't cause streaks in the baked custards.) Freeze the ramekins until the syrup is firm and doesn't stick to your finger when you touch it, about 15 minutes.

5. When the custard base and the ramekins are ready, preheat the oven to 325°F. Put the ramekins in a deep-sided casserole dish and pour water into the dish until it comes about one-third of the way up the sides of the ramekins. Divide the custard base evenly among the ramekins; each ramekin will get a scant ½ cup. Cover the casserole dish tightly with aluminum foil, then use a paring knife to poke three slits into each corner of the foil to let out some of the steam.

6. Bake the custards for 50 to 60 minutes, turning the dish 180 degrees halfway through the baking time so they bake evenly. Check the custards by lifting up one edge of the foil and jiggling the casserole dish; the custard should wiggle a bit but not slosh around.

7. When the custards are fully baked, remove them from the oven, discard the foil, and set them out on a counter to cool to room temperature; the custards should not look at all liquid and should barely jiggle when you shake them. Cover the custards with plastic wrap and refrigerate them for at least 4 hours to finish setting before serving. ★

Make Ahead
The baked custards can be kept in the refrigerator for up to 5 days.

Serving Suggestion
Coconut Whipped Cream (recipe follows)

Above and Beyond
Coconut Whipped Cream
2 cups heavy cream
¼ cup granulated sugar
1 cup unsweetened shredded coconut

In a medium saucepan, heat the cream and sugar until the mixture is steaming, stirring frequently to keep the sugar from sticking to the bottom of the pot. Turn off the heat and add the coconut, then let the mixture sit and steep for 1 hour. Strain the cream through a fine-mesh sieve to remove the coconut. Refrigerate the coconut-flavored cream until it is very cold, then whip the cream to soft peaks. ★

Bubbles on the surface of the custards before they're baked can mar the finished puddings. Just before you put them in the oven, break up the bubbles by passing the very tip of the flame from a kitchen torch over the top of the puddings or by running the corner of a paper towel over the tops of the custards.

Chocolate Mousse

Makes 6 mousses

This chocolate mousse is light and creamy and smooth. It's wonderful served on its own but we also use it to make our Chocolate Mousse Cake (page 61). To keep the mousse as airy as possible, we whip the cream and whip the eggs, then fold everything together. (As with all our recipes that use uncooked egg, we use pasteurized eggs when we make this mousse in our cafés.)

1¾ cups heavy cream

10 ounces dark chocolate (preferably 70% cacao), coarsely chopped

2 extra-large eggs

1 extra-large egg yolk

½ cup plus 2½ tablespoons granulated sugar

¼ cup water

1. In the bowl of a stand mixer fitted with the whisk attachment, whip the cream on medium until it holds medium peaks. Transfer the whipped cream to a large bowl, cover with plastic wrap, and refrigerate to keep cool. Clean the mixer bowl and whisk and dry them thoroughly.

2. Melt the chocolate in the top of a double boiler, stirring to keep it from burning, or microwave it in 20-second intervals, stirring after each interval, until it becomes liquid. Set aside.

3. In the clean bowl of the stand mixer fitted with the clean whisk attachment, whip the eggs and egg yolks together on high until very frothy and pale, about 2 minutes. (Do not overwhip or the eggs will start to break down.) In a small saucepan, bring the sugar and water to a boil over high heat, stirring occasionally. Let it boil for 1 minute. With the mixer on low, pour the sugar syrup into the eggs in a thin, steady stream about the width of a pencil, making sure not to pour it onto the sides of a bowl, where it will stick and solidify. Turn the mixer to high and whip everything together until the side of the mixing bowl has cooled to room temperature, about 5 minutes; the mixture will be thick and sticky-looking.

4. With the mixer on low, slowly add the melted chocolate. Remove the bowl from the mixer and finish mixing and folding in the chocolate by hand with a rubber spatula.

5. Add the chocolate mixture to the bowl of chilled whipped cream and use the rubber spatula to gently fold and mix all the ingredients together until combined, making sure there are no hidden pockets of cream.

6. Divide the mousse among six serving cups and chill before serving. ★

Make Ahead
The finished mousse can be refrigerated, covered with plastic wrap, for 3 to 4 days.

Serving Suggestion
Vanilla Whipped Cream (page 160) and fresh raspberries

Frozen White Chocolate Raspberry Mousse

Makes 8 mousses

This beautiful, pink-hued mousse was one of the desserts we served on the very first day we opened The Chocolate Room, and it remains one of our favorite ways to use white chocolate. The tartness of the raspberries offsets the sweet, milky quality of the chocolate, and freezing the mixture makes it not only light and creamy but also cool and refreshing. This mousse uses a little bit of gelatin instead of egg whites, so it's very simple to make, and it should be served directly out of the freezer so that it doesn't melt before it's eaten.

⅓ cup raspberry liqueur, such as Chambord

1 tablespoon powdered gelatin

24 ounces fresh or frozen raspberries

½ cup granulated sugar

12 ounces white chocolate, coarsely chopped

2 cups heavy cream

1 teaspoon pure vanilla extract

¾ cup confectioners' sugar

8 heaping tablespoons Chocolate Cookie Crumbs (optional, see page 78)

1. In a medium saucepan, stir together the raspberry liqueur and gelatin. Set aside at room temperature for 10 minutes to bloom the gelatin. Add the raspberries and granulated sugar to the saucepan and cook over medium-high heat, stirring and mashing the berries with a whisk, until the sugar and the gelatin have dissolved, the raspberries are warm and liquid, and the mixture begins to bubble.

2. Remove from the heat, add the white chocolate, and let the mixture sit while the chocolate melts, about 5 minutes. Whisk the mixture until it looks uniform, then let cool to room temperature. Strain the mixture through a fine-mesh sieve into a large bowl, pressing it through with a rubber spatula so only the raspberry seeds remain in the sieve. Put the mixture in the refrigerator to chill for a few minutes. (If you refrigerate the mixture for longer than 5 minutes, make sure to whisk it every few minutes so the gelatin doesn't set.)

3. In the bowl of a stand mixer fitted with the whisk attachment, combine the cream, vanilla, and confectioners' sugar and whip on medium-low until the cream holds medium peaks, about 3 minutes. Add the whipped cream to the chilled raspberry mixture and fold them together until everything is thoroughly incorporated and no streaks remain.

4. Put 1 heaping tablespoon of the cookie crumbs, if using, into the bottom of each of eight serving cups. Divide the raspberry mousse among the cups and freeze them for at least 4 hours, preferably overnight. Serve frozen. ★

Make Ahead
The frozen puddings can be kept in the freezer, covered with plastic wrap, for up to 2 weeks.

Serving Suggestion
Fresh raspberries

Sticky Date Pudding with Chocolate Toffee Sauce

Makes 6 puddings

Dates have been a major crop in Southern California since the turn of the twentieth century, when "agricultural explorers" hired by the Department of Agriculture brought them to California's Coachella Valley. As luck would have it, the country was in the midst of an "Arabian" craze, and the industry capitalized on the fruit's origins—local towns were renamed Oasis, Arabia, and Mecca, and shops sold sweets and desserts made from the fruit. These days dates are no longer considered an exotic specialty, but California still produces about 50 million pounds of them every year.

These date puddings are based on the sticky toffee puddings that are popular in the U.K. and Australia. We've adjusted the recipe to suit our tastes and added chocolate to the toffee sauce. The result is moist and sticky and sweet—just like the dates themselves. Pictured on page 106.

Date Puddings

½ cup plus 1 tablespoon all-purpose flour

½ teaspoon baking powder

Pinch of salt

1 extra-large egg

½ teaspoon pure vanilla extract

3 ounces dried dates, pitted and quartered

¾ cup water

½ teaspoon baking soda

2 tablespoons unsalted butter, at room temperature

½ cup granulated sugar

Vegetable oil spray

Chocolate-Toffee Sauce

5 tablespoons unsalted butter

½ cup light brown sugar

¼ cup heavy cream

1 ounce dark chocolate (preferably 60% cacao), coarsely chopped

Special Tools

Six 4-ounce (½-cup) ceramic ramekins (3¾ inches in diameter) (see page 17)

Make the Puddings

1. Preheat the oven to 350°F. In a medium bowl, mix together the flour, baking powder, and salt. In a small bowl, combine the egg and vanilla. Set both bowls aside.

2. In a small saucepan, combine the dates and water and bring the water to a rolling boil. Boil for 2 minutes to soften the dates. Transfer the mixture to a blender and blend into a thick puree. Return the puree to the saucepan and reheat until it just begins to bubble; remove from the heat. Add the baking soda and stir to incorporate. Let cool to room temperature.

3. In the bowl of a stand mixer fitted with the paddle attachment, combine the butter and granulated sugar and mix on low until the ingredients begin to come together, then beat on medium-high for 3 minutes, stopping frequently to scrape down the sides and bottom of the bowl.

4. Turn the mixer to low and add the egg and vanilla, then mix on low until just combined. Use a rubber spatula to scrape down the sides and bottom of the bowl, then beat on high for 1 minute, until the mixture is smooth and homogenous. Add the flour mixture to the bowl and mix on low until just incorporated, then scrape down the

sides and bottom of the bowl; mix for 10 seconds to combine. Add the date mixture and mix on low until just incorporated, about 20 seconds.

5. Remove the bowl from the mixer and finish mixing by hand to ensure that all the ingredients are evenly incorporated.

6. Spray six ramekins with vegetable oil spray and divide the batter evenly among them; each ramekin will get a scant ¼ cup batter. Place the filled ramekins in a roasting pan or casserole dish and fill the outer pan with ¾ inch of water. Bake the puddings in the water bath, uncovered, until a paring knife inserted into the center of a pudding comes out clean, about 40 minutes. Remove the puddings from the oven and let cool for a few minutes; they should be served warm.

Make the Sauce

In a medium saucepan, combine the butter, brown sugar, and cream and cook over medium heat until the butter has melted, the sugar has dissolved, and the mixture is boiling. Remove from the heat and add the chocolate. Let the mixture sit for 1 minute to melt the chocolate, then whisk everything together to form a smooth sauce.

Assemble the Puddings

When the puddings are cool enough to handle and the sauce is ready, flip each pudding onto a serving plate; they should slide out of the ramekins easily. Top each pudding with about ¼ cup of the toffee sauce and serve immediately. ★

Make Ahead

The baked puddings can be refrigerated for up to 5 days and reheated in the microwave for 20 to 30 seconds. The Chocolate-Toffee Sauce can be refrigerated for up to 1 week and reheated in a pot on the stove or by microwaving it in 30-second intervals, stirring after each interval, until it is warm and fluid.

Chocolate Almond Flan

Makes one 9-inch flan

Cool, creamy, eggy flan is one of the most classic desserts in Latin America, and in the last half-century it has become popular in the parts of the United States with a large Hispanic population—not to mention ubiquitous in Mexican restaurants across the country. When our executive pastry chef, Carmine Arroyo, was a kid, his family would make flan in big cake pans and leave it in the refrigerator to be served throughout the week, cut into thick slices.

The version Carmine makes here at The Chocolate Room uses cocoa mixed in with the rest of the ingredients to give the whole pudding a rich chocolate flavor. He also adds almond extract—one of his favorite flavors to pair with chocolate—which turns what is usually a homey dessert into something surprisingly sophisticated.

2½ cups granulated sugar

2 tablespoons water

4 teaspoons light corn syrup

8 extra-large eggs

4 cups whole milk

1 cup heavy cream

¼ cup plus 2 tablespoons unsweetened Dutch-process cocoa powder

2 teaspoons pure almond extract

The ingredients for the flan have to be whisked together by hand because using a mixer would introduce too much air and create bubbles in the flan. To stabilize the bowl so that it won't move around on the counter as you whisk, twist a kitchen towel into a long rope, form it into a ring on the kitchen counter, and nestle your mixing bowl into the ring.

recipe continues on the next page

1. Preheat the oven to 325°F. In a medium saucepan, combine ¾ cup of the sugar, the water, and corn syrup. Use a wet paper towel to wipe down the sides of the pot and have a cup of water with a pastry brush nearby. Bring the mixture to a vigorous boil over high heat. If sugar crystals form on the sides of the pan, brush them down with the wet pastry brush. When the sugar syrup begins to take on a golden hue along the edges, reduce the heat to low so it doesn't cook too quickly. Continue to cook, shaking the pan frequently to distribute the cooked sugar, until the caramel has a dark golden, almost orange color, then immediately remove the pan from the heat and pour the caramel into the bottom of a 9-inch cake pan. Let the caramel sit until it cools down and becomes fairly firm.

2. In a large bowl, whisk the eggs to break them up. Add the remaining 1¾ cups sugar and whisk until well combined; set aside.

3. In a medium saucepan, combine the milk and cream and cook over medium-high heat until they start to steam. Remove from the heat, add the cocoa powder, and whisk well, scraping down the sides of the saucepan to break up any small pockets of cocoa, until all the cocoa has dissolved into the milk.

4. While whisking, pour the hot milk mixture into the eggs in a slow, steady stream to temper the eggs. Add the almond extract and whisk well to combine.

5. Pour the custard base over the caramel in the cake pan, and put the filled cake pan into a baking pan at least ½ inch taller than the cake pan. Fill the outer pan with about ¾ inch of water, then cover the whole thing with aluminum foil. (Make sure the foil is pulled tight and won't sag over the flan.)

6. Bake for 1 hour and 30 minutes, until the flan is just set but still looks wet and jiggles when the pan is moved. (You can touch the top of the flan very gently with your finger to make sure that it is set; some of the custard may come off on your finger, but it will be thick, not liquid.) Keep the flan in the water bath and set aside to cool; the residual heat of the water will continue to cook the flan, and it will set as it cools. Once the flan cools to room temperature, refrigerate it for at least 3 hours to firm up.

7. To unmold the flan, run a paring knife between the sides of the flan and the pan, then place a large serving plate upside down on top of the cake pan and flip the flan onto the plate. (The plate should have a raised edge and be big enough to hold any caramel that slides off the top of the flan and falls down the sides.) Heat the bottom of the pan very quickly with a kitchen torch or soak a kitchen towel in very hot water, wring it out, and place on the bottom of the pan to loosen the caramel. Gently remove the pan. If any of the caramel has solidified into glasslike pieces, remove them from the flan and discard. Slice and serve. ★

Make Ahead
The baked flan can be kept in the refrigerator for up to 5 days.

Fondue

Makes 6 servings

 tip

Before you serve the fondue, preheat the serving bowl by filling it with hot water for a minute.

Place **6 ounces coarsely chopped dark chocolate (preferably 60% cacao)** in a heatproof bowl and set aside. In a small saucepan, heat **¼ cup heavy cream** and **¼ cup water** over medium heat until they are steaming, then pour the hot liquid over the chocolate and whisk everything together until the chocolate has melted and the fondue is smooth.

Fruit + Treats For Dipping
(use any combination of the following)
Strawberries
Bananas, halved lengthwise
Pineapple, sliced
Mini Macaroons (not dipped in chocolate, page 79)
Graham Crackers (not dipped in chocolate, page 82)
Chocolate Stout Gingerbread (page 67), cubed
Chocolate Marshmallows (page 141)

1 Serve the fondue in a ceramic fondue pot.

2 Place a lit candle underneath to keep the chocolate fluid.

3 Serve the fruit, baked goods, and/or marshmallows on the side, with long-handled forks to use for dipping.

Make Ahead
The fondue can be kept in the refrigerator for up to 10 days and reheated in a hot water bath or by microwaving it in 30-second intervals, stirring well after each interval, until liquid. If the fondue separates when it cools, use an immersion blender to make it smooth again after reheating.

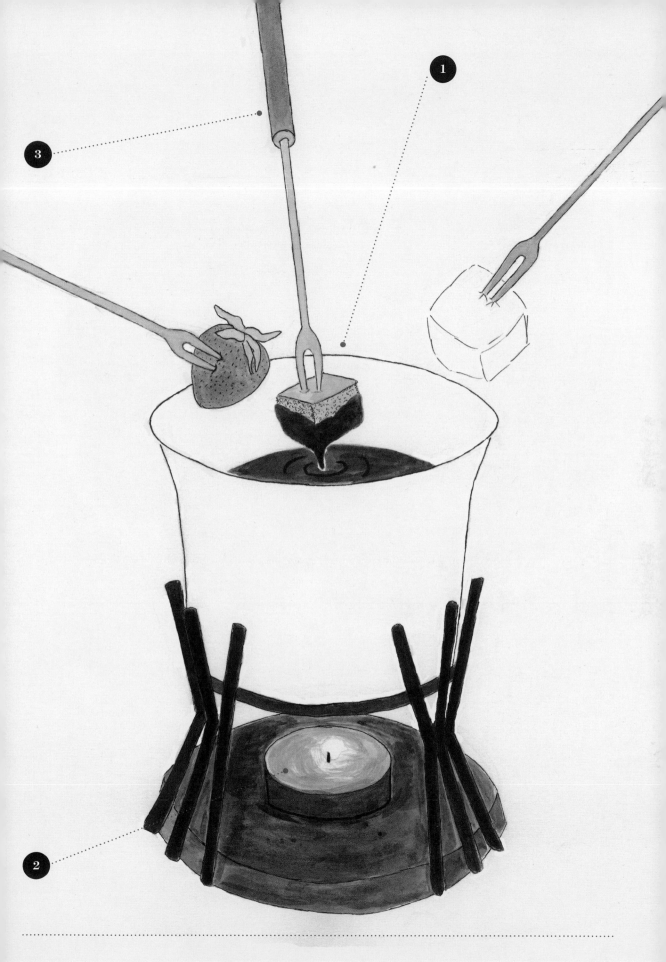

Peanut Butter Cups
recipe on page 134

**Milk Chocolate
Almond Clusters**
recipe on page 132

Caramel Turtles
recipe on page 136

confections

How to Temper Chocolate— A Few Simple Methods

When you melt chocolate—so that you can drizzle it, dip caramels into it, or turn it into any kind of confection—you break down its molecular structure. If you simply let the melted chocolate cool and harden up on its own, the chocolate's fats and proteins won't align themselves correctly, and you'll get white, dusty-looking streaks of cocoa fat (called "bloom") instead of nice shiny chocolate. The process of tempering chocolate coaxes the molecules back into alignment so that when the chocolate hardens, you get the look and texture you're used to.

Tempering chocolate can actually be quite simple: all you have to do is heat some of your chocolate until it's fluid, then mix in some hard, unmelted chocolate (which will have already been tempered by the chocolate company). The heated chocolate will attach itself to the hard chocolate and fall into the correct molecular alignment.

So why is tempering considered so hard? Basically, it takes time and patience (and a little elbow grease). If you rush or try to take shortcuts, it may not work. Also, environmental factors like hot or moist weather can interfere with the tempering process (see "Common Problems," page 128).

Here are a few ways to heat and cool the chocolate and a guide to the appropriate melting and working temperatures of different kinds of chocolate. Once you find a tempering method that you like and that gives you nice, consistent results, stick with it. Tempering isn't actually all that hard—you just need patience and a tiny bit of luck.

Microwave Method

 Take the chocolate you need for your recipe, in pastilles or chopped into pieces roughly ½ to 1 inch square, and divide it into three parts. (It's good to have some extra sitting by, just in case you need it.)

 Put two-thirds of the chocolate in a microwave-safe bowl made of a material that won't hold heat for very long; microwave-safe plastic or thin Pyrex is ideal, ceramic is not.

 Microwave the chocolate in the bowl in 20-second bursts, stirring it with a rubber spatula and scraping the sides and bottom of the bowl in between bursts so that none of it burns. (If melting white chocolate, use 10-second bursts.)

 When the chocolate is thin and fluid, set the bowl on the counter to begin the tempering process: add a few pieces of the hard, unmelted chocolate to the bowl and stir the whole thing with a rubber spatula until the hard chocolate melts; the motion of the spatula will agitate the melted chocolate and help it start to form the correct molecular bonds.

 Continue adding the hard chocolate, a few pieces at a time, and stirring them in until they have melted; make sure to scrape the sides and bottom of the bowl as you stir because that's where the chocolate is likely to cool the fastest.

❻ Once the chocolate has cooled a little and it is taking a long time for the newly added pieces to melt, stop adding chocolate and start checking the temperature of the mixture with a good candy thermometer (ideally a digital one, which will be more accurate). Continue stirring until the melted chocolate has reached the appropriate tempered temperature, as indicated on the Tempering Chart (page 129).

7

Test the chocolate to see if it is tempered: dip a knife or a small offset spatula into the chocolate and set it aside somewhere cool and dry to firm up. Tempered chocolate will be shiny when hard and will break with a clean, clear snap.

8

Once the chocolate has reached the appropriate temperature, you'll want to raise the chocolate up a few degrees to the working temperature on the chart by microwaving it for 10 seconds, then stirring thoroughly with the rubber spatula; this makes the chocolate easier to work with. You can repeat this process at any point while you're working with the chocolate if it becomes too stiff.

9

If there are still unincorporated pieces of chocolate in your bowl after you've finished the tempering process, remove them from the bowl and discard them.

Pros of This Method

If your microwave is in a convenient place in your kitchen, this is a very simple way to heat chocolate without needing a pot or other tools. Also, unlike the Stovetop Method (right), this method does not involve any water, so you don't run the risk of ruining the chocolate.

Cons of This Method

This method requires a microwave-proof bowl that is big enough to fit the chocolate but small enough for your microwave, and if your microwave is in a slightly inaccessible location (like below the counter), it can involve a lot of bending and/or reaching.

Stovetop Method

1

Take the chocolate you need for your recipe, in pastilles or chopped into pieces roughly ½ to 1 inch square, and divide it into three parts. (It's good to have some extra sitting by, just in case you need it.)

2

Put a large, heatproof bowl on top of a medium-sized pot half-filled with water, and bring the water to a boil, then lower the heat so the water is only simmering. (The bowl should be made of a material that won't hold heat for very long; metal or thin Pyrex is ideal, ceramic is not. The rim of the bowl should also be much larger than the top of the pot so that the bowl sits well above the water and the boiling water doesn't touch the bottom of the bowl.)

3

When the water is ready, put two-thirds of the chocolate in the bowl and allow it to melt, stirring the chocolate frequently with a rubber spatula and scraping the sides and bottom of the bowl so that none of it burns.

4

When the chocolate is thin and fluid, remove from the heat and set the bowl on the counter to begin the tempering process: add a few pieces of the hard, unmelted chocolate to the bowl and stir the whole thing with a rubber spatula until the hard chocolate melts; the motion of the spatula will agitate the melted chocolate and help it start to form the correct molecular bonds.

5

Continue adding the hard chocolate, a few pieces at a time, and stirring them in until they have melted; make sure to scrape the sides and bottom of the bowl as you stir because that's where the chocolate is likely to cool the fastest.

6

Once the chocolate has cooled a little and it is taking a long time for the newly added pieces to melt, stop adding chocolate and start checking the temperature of the mixture with a good candy thermometer (ideally a digital one, which will be more accurate). Continue stirring until the melted chocolate has reached the appropriate tempered temperature, as indicated on the Tempering Chart (page 129).

Test the chocolate to see if it is tempered: dip a knife or a small offset spatula into the chocolate and set it aside somewhere cool and dry to firm up. Tempered chocolate will be shiny when hard and will break with a clean, clear snap.

Once the chocolate has reached the appropriate temperature, you'll want to raise the chocolate up a few degrees to the working temperature on the chart (opposite) by putting it back over simmering water for a few seconds, stirring thoroughly with the rubber spatula; this makes the chocolate easier to work with. You can repeat this process at any point while you're working with the chocolate if it becomes too stiff.

If there are still unincorporated pieces of chocolate in your bowl after you've finished the tempering process, remove them from the bowl and discard them.

Pros of This Method
This method can be done without a microwave-safe bowl and doesn't require you to put the chocolate in and out of a microwave, so it can be more convenient for some kitchen set-ups.

Cons of This Method
Because of the steam generated by the simmering water, you run the risk of getting some steam or water into the chocolate. If any moisture gets into the chocolate, it will ruin it, and no amount of tempering can fix it.

Ways to Cool Chocolate Faster

The safest, most effective way of cooling tempering chocolate is to simply stir it with a rubber spatula, scraping the sides of the bowl, as described above. If you're anxious about time, however, there are a few ways to speed up the process.

Immersion Blender
Using an immersion blender to mix the melted chocolate with the tempered pieces can speed up the cooling process as long as you remember to stop and scrape the sides and bottom of the bowl with a rubber spatula. The blender will, however, incorporate air into the chocolate, and if there is any moisture in the air, this can ruin the chocolate.

Cold Packs
If the bowl you are tempering the chocolate in is retaining too much heat, or if you just want to speed the cooling process a little bit, you can place a couple of cold packs (or a couple bags of frozen peas) along the outside of the bowl. In doing this, however, you run the risk of cooling the chocolate too quickly, and it can reach the tempered temperature before the proteins and fats have

realigned properly, so be sure to scrape the cold parts of the bowl frequently.

Ice Bath
If you want to try to cool the chocolate rapidly, you can put the bowl filled with chocolate in a bowl full of ice. In doing this, however, you run the risk of cooling the chocolate too quickly, and it can reach the tempered temperature before the proteins and fats have realigned properly. You also run the risk of getting moisture into the chocolate and ruining it.

Common Problems
Bloom
The main problem that occurs when you temper chocolate is that it can "bloom," causing white streaks or dots to appear on your cooled, hardened chocolate. There are two causes of bloom.

The first, "fat bloom," happens if the chocolate isn't agitated and stirred enough while it's tempering and its molecular structure doesn't come together perfectly. When this happens, the fat appears as long white streaks on the chocolate. If this happens and you haven't mixed the chocolate with any other ingredients, you can just start over by bringing it all back to melting temperature and adding more hard (tempered) chocolate.

The second, "moisture bloom," happens if any water comes into contact with the chocolate while you're tempering. When this happens, the chocolate will look spotted or like it has a layer of dust on its surface. If this happens, you won't be able to temper this chocolate, but you can save it and use it when you'll need to add melted chocolate to butter, milk, or cream—when you're making brownies, ganache, or ice cream, for instance.

Unfortunately, it's impossible to tell if your chocolate will bloom until it hardens, which is why we test the temper before we use the melted chocolate. (See the instructions in the tempering methods above.)

Burnt Chocolate

Just one little bit of burnt chocolate will infuse an entire bowl with an acrid flavor. To keep the chocolate from burning, make sure to stir it as you heat it, scraping the sides and bottom of the bowl well.

Weather-Related Problems

When tempering chocolate, the ideal setting is a cool, dry room.

If the weather is too hot (or you've heated up your kitchen by using the oven), the chocolate can take too long to firm up and can fall out of temper as it cools. If this happens, you'll end up with fat bloom on the chocolate.

If the weather is humid or you have water on your bowl or your rubber spatula, the water can get into the chocolate and cause it to "seize" and become thick and goopy.

Tempering Chart

The following temperatures should work for most chocolate, but if the chocolate you use comes with specific information about what temperatures to use, follow those instructions.

Type of Chocolate	Working Temperature	Tempered Temperature	Melting Temperature
Dark Chocolate	87 to 88°F	82°F	118 to 120°F
Milk Chocolate	85 to 88°F	79°F	110 to 118°F
White Chocolate	85 to 88°F	79°F	110 to 118°F

The last few degrees before chocolate reaches its tempered temperature always seem to take forever, but they are the most critical, so be patient and continue stirring until the chocolate has cooled to the appropriate temperature.

Chocolate Caramel Popcorn

Makes about 15 cups

Our take on this classic ballpark treat is rich and decadent. Instead of using a thin candy coating, we make a rich, flavorful caramel and coat each popped kernel of corn with a thick layer of it. (To really coat the popcorn well, we put it and the caramel into a heated oven a few times to keep the caramel from firming up to quickly.) Then we drizzle the caramel corn with enough semisweet chocolate to cover every piece of popcorn, and break the whole thing into large, satisfying chunks. This treat is particularly popular around the holidays—our customers buy so much of it that we make multiple batches every day and still can't keep up with the demand.

1 tablespoon vegetable oil

½ cup unpopped popcorn kernels

1¼ cups granulated sugar

¾ cup water

1 tablespoon light corn syrup

6 tablespoons (¾ stick) unsalted butter

½ teaspoon salt

½ teaspoon baking soda

16 ounces dark chocolate (preferably 60% cacao)

1. Preheat the oven to 350°F. In a large pot with a lid, heat the oil and popcorn kernels over medium heat, shaking the pot occasionally, until the kernels pop. Remove from the heat when the popping sounds slow down to one every 2 or 3 seconds so you don't burn the popcorn. Transfer the popcorn to a large metal bowl or a deep, oven-proof casserole dish, and remove any remaining unpopped kernels or burned bits; set aside.

tip

If any of the popcorn burns, the acrid flavor will permeate the whole batch; it's better to have too many unpopped kernels (which can be reused) than to risk burning even one piece of popcorn.

2. In a medium-large saucepan, combine the sugar, water, and corn syrup. Use a wet paper towel to wipe down the sides of the pot and have a cup of water with a pastry brush nearby. Bring the mixture to a vigorous boil over high heat. If sugar crystals form on the sides of the pan, brush them down with the wet pastry brush. When the sugar syrup begins to take on a golden hue along the edges, reduce the heat to medium-low so it doesn't cook too quickly, and cook, shaking the pot frequently to distribute the cooked sugar, until the caramel has a dark golden color, then immediately remove from the heat. Add the butter, baking soda, and salt, standing back from the saucepan to avoid the steam. Stir in the butter until it is evenly distributed and the caramel has taken on an orange hue.

3. Pour the caramel over the popcorn and stir it with a rubber spatula. When the caramel becomes too stiff to work with, put the entire bowl in the oven and let it heat for 3 minutes to soften the caramel, then remove and continue to stir. Repeat this process until all the popcorn is at least partially coated with caramel, scraping the bottom of the bowl each time to make sure you're using any caramel that has pooled there.

recipe continues on the next page

4. Line a sheet pan with parchment paper, pour the caramel-coated popcorn onto the pan, and use the rubber spatula to spread and press the popcorn into one layer. Set the popcorn aside to cool.

5. When the popcorn has cooled to room temperature, temper the chocolate using any of the tempering techniques listed on page 126, then bring it up to working temperature. When the chocolate is ready, divide it between two pastry bags. Cut a small hole in the end of one bag and drizzle the chocolate across the top of the popcorn in a zigzag pattern. When you reach the end of the tray, repeat the zigzag pattern in the opposite direction so that you create an uneven crosshatch pattern; you should use all the chocolate in the first bag. Set the pan in a cool place until the chocolate has set enough that it is firm to the touch (to speed up this process, you can put the tray in the refrigerator for a minute). Flip the entire slab of popcorn so that the chocolate-covered side is down, and drizzle the other side of the popcorn with the second bag of chocolate. (If the chocolate stiffens up too much while the first side is setting, it can be heated for 5 to 10 seconds in the microwave or over a saucepan of hot water to bring it back to working temperature.) Set the popcorn aside to let the chocolate solidify. When the chocolate has set, break the popcorn into large chunks. ★

Make Ahead
The finished popcorn will stay fresh in an airtight container or cellophane bag, if it's well sealed, at room temperature for 2 to 3 weeks.

Above and Beyond
Spiced Caramel Popcorn
Add 1 teaspoon ancho chile powder and ½ teaspoon chipotle chile powder when you add the salt, baking soda, and butter to the caramel. The chile can become fragrant as it heats up, so stand back from the pot so it won't irritate your eyes. ★

Milk Chocolate Almond Clusters

Makes about 55 clusters

This confection is just as simple as it is delicious. It's a mixture of tempered milk chocolate with sliced almonds and a generous amount of feuilletine, an ingredient that has the texture of broken-up wafer cookies and the flavor of a fantastic breakfast cereal. The key to making these clusters is to keep them loose, with lots of jagged, spiky edges; that way the whole thing stays really crunchy and easy to bite into. Pictured on page 124.

4 cups feuilletine (see below)

2 cups sliced almonds

32 ounces milk chocolate

Special Tools
¾-ounce (1½-tablespoon) cookie scoop (optional, see page 19)

Feuilletine, which is made up of crispy pastry flakes, is not readily available in grocery stores, but it can be ordered from a number of online stores that specialize in pastry ingredients (see page 21).

1. In a large bowl, mix together the feuilletine and almonds. Temper the chocolate using any of the tempering techniques listed on page 126, then bring it back to working temperature. When the chocolate is ready, pour it onto the almond mixture and use a rubber spatula to gently fold everything together until all the feuilletine and almonds are coated. (Some of the almonds' white edges may be peeking through.) If the chocolate stiffens up too much before you're done mixing, the entire mixture can be heated for 5 to 10 seconds in the microwave or over a saucepan of hot water.

2. Line two sheet pans with parchment paper and use two large spoons or a ¾-ounce (1½-tablespoon) cookie scoop to scoop out loose clumps of the chocolate-almond mixture and set them on the parchment. The clusters should be roughly 1½ inches in diameter and should fall apart slightly on the pan so that the texture of the almonds and feuilletine shows through the chocolate. Set the pans aside in a cool, dry place to let the chocolate set. ★

Make Ahead
The milk chocolate almond clusters can be stored in an airtight container at room temperature for 2 weeks or longer.

Cookie Chip Chocolates

Makes about 50 chocolates

These whimsical confections were dreamed up and created at The Chocolate Room. When we began making our own chocolate confections in-house, Jon, who has always loved to play with words, came up with the idea of doing an inverted chocolate chip cookie—instead of chocolate chips stirred into cookie dough, we would make crisp cookie chips and enrobe them in rich, semisweet chocolate. The result is a cookie-lover's confection and one of our favorite treats of all time.

½ recipe dough from Chocolate Chip Cookies (page 71), without the chocolate added, chilled for at least 4 hours, preferably overnight

32 ounces dark chocolate (preferably 60% cacao)

Special Tools
¾-ounce (1½-tablespoon) cookie scoop (optional, see page 19)

1. Preheat the oven to 350°F. Line two sheet pans with parchment paper or silicone liners. Divide the chilled dough in half and put one half on each prepared pan. Press the dough into a very thin disk, then use a long offset spatula or a rubber spatula and a butter knife to spread the dough out into a sheet about 10 inches wide by 15 inches long. The dough will be very thin and sticky—smooth it into as even a layer as possible. Bake the dough for 5 minutes, then rotate the pans and bake for another 5 minutes, until the dough is cooked through but still quite soft and the edges have started to brown a bit.

recipe continues on the next page

2. Turn off the oven and remove one of the sheets of cookie dough; leave the other in the oven to keep warm. (The key to making the cookie chips is to cut them while they're warm so that they don't shatter under the knife.) Slide the first sheet of baked cookie dough onto a large cutting board and use a chef's knife to cut it into ¼-inch squares. (The pieces don't have to be uniform.) Set the cookie chips aside to cool to room temperature. Repeat with the other sheet.

3. When the cookie chips are completely cool, temper the chocolate using any of the tempering techniques listed on page 126, then bring it back to working temperature. When the chocolate is ready, add the cookie chips and use a rubber spatula to gently fold everything together until all the cookie chips are coated. If the chocolate stiffens up too much before you're done mixing, the entire mixture can be heated for 5 to 10 seconds in the microwave or over a saucepan of hot water.

4. Line three sheet pans with parchment paper and use two large spoons or a ¾-ounce (1½-tablespoon) cookie scoop to scoop out loose clumps of the chocolate-cookie mixture and set them on the parchment. The clusters should be roughly 1½ inches in diameter; press them a little bit with the back of the spoon or scoop to flatten them slightly, so the texture of the cookie chips shows through the chocolate. Set the pans aside in a cool, dry place to let the chocolate set. ★

Make Ahead

The cookie chips can be stored in an airtight container at room temperature for up to 5 days. The finished confections can be stored in an airtight container at room temperature for up to 2 weeks.

Peanut Butter Cups

Makes 72 peanut butter cups

These peanut butter–filled confections are inspired by the classic candy created by H. B. Reese in the 1920s, but our version (pictured on page 124) is a bit creamier than the original, with a purer peanut flavor and a dark chocolate shell that offsets the sweetness of the filling. This is one of the more complex confections we make, so we usually make it over a couple of days so that the peanut fudge and the chocolate have enough time to cool, and set up properly. Like most shaped confections, these are made in firm plastic chocolate molds; if the chocolate is tempered properly, it shrinks up a bit as it hardens and pulls away from the plastic so that the finished cups slide right out of the mold. If you don't want to use candy molds, you can use this filling to make chocolate-dipped peanut butter truffles (see Alternate Method, page 136).

¾ cup heavy cream

2 tablespoons light corn syrup

1½ cups granulated sugar

½ cup dark brown sugar

¼ teaspoon salt

2 tablespoons unsalted butter

¾ cup natural creamy peanut butter with salt

½ teaspoon pure vanilla extract

5 pounds dark chocolate (preferably 60% cacao)

Special Tools

Polycarbonate chocolate mold with fluted round 38 x 19-mm indentations, enough for 72 peanut butter cups (see page 20; optional)

Large cooling rack or wire pan grate (see page 17)

When you heat the cream and sugar for the peanut butter fudge, have a tub of cold water nearby to clean the thermometer immediately, so that the sugar doesn't stick to it.

1. In a medium saucepan, combine the cream, corn syrup, granulated sugar, brown sugar, and salt and whisk to break up any clumps of brown sugar. Add the butter and bring the mixture to a boil over medium-high heat, stirring occasionally with the whisk.

2. Once the mixture begins to boil, attach a candy thermometer to the side of the pan and cook until the mixture reaches 240°F, then remove from the heat. Transfer the mixture to a heat-resistant bowl and set it aside to cool to around 180°F, 15 to 20 minutes. The mixture will begin to solidify on top and will be thick and sticky.

 tip

When cooking the peanut butter fudge, avoid stirring the mixture too much, as this could create sugar crystals that would give the fudge a grainy texture.

3. Transfer the sugar mixture to the bowl of a stand mixer fitted with the paddle attachment, add the peanut butter and vanilla, and mix on low until the sugar cools enough that the mixture loses its sticky appearance, solidifies, and begins to form a ball, about 2 minutes. The fudge should lose the sheen of peanut oil on its surface and have a dry texture. (Overmixing the fudge could also cause the oil to separate out of the mixture.) If the fudge begins to look crumbly, stop the mixer and knead it with your hands to make it smooth.

4. Transfer the fudge to a storage container, press down on the top to create a flat surface, and press parchment paper directly against the surface to absorb excess oils. Let the fudge cool completely.

5. When the fudge is cool, temper 4½ pounds of the chocolate using a very large bowl and any of the tempering techniques listed on page 126, then bring it back to working temperature. Fill the candy molds with the chocolate, working with one tray of molds at a time. Hold the candy mold over the tempering bowl and use a ladle to fill it with

chocolate, holding the mold at an angle so any excess chocolate can slide back into the bowl. The chocolate can be reheated for 10 to 15 seconds in the microwave or over a saucepan of hot water as necessary to keep it at working temperature. When all the indentations are full of chocolate, use a bench scraper, metal spatula, or the edge of a cleaver to scrape the top and sides of the mold to remove any chocolate that is not inside the indentations. Use a wooden spoon to hit the sides of the mold a couple dozen times so that the chocolate settles into all the corners of the mold and any air bubbles are released.

6. Flip the mold upside down over the tempering bowl, and hit the back of the mold a few dozen times with the wooden spoon so that most of the chocolate drips back into the bowl, leaving just a thin coating inside each of the indentations. Use the scraper to remove any excess chocolate that is sitting on the top of the mold, then set it upside down on a large wire rack for 10 minutes. Scrape the tops of the mold once again to remove excess chocolate. Repeat until all the molds have been filled.

7. Set the filled molds aside for at least 4 hours to firm up. Pour the remaining tempered chocolate onto a parchment paper–lined sheet pan and set aside to firm up.

8. When the chocolate has set, use a teaspoon or a ⅛-ounce cookie scoop to portion out 1 to 1½ teaspoons of peanut butter fudge for each peanut butter cup (the exact amount will depend on how thick the chocolate in the mold is and how much room is left). Roll the fudge into little balls and set them in the lined molds, pressing them down so they don't stick out of the indentations.

9. Melt the leftover chocolate. Use the remaining ½ pound hard chocolate to temper the chocolate using any method described on page 126, then bring the chocolate back up to working temperature. Hold a filled mold over the tempering bowl and use a ladle to fill the remaining space with

recipe continues on the next page

Chocolate Peppermint Bark
recipe on page 140

Chocolate Bark

Makes 1 sheet pan of chocolate bark

This is one of the simplest-looking recipes we have at The Chocolate Room, but it's actually a very carefully calibrated confection. Every batch must have the right balance of ingredients so that the slight sweetness of the almonds offsets the bitterness of the chocolate, and the sea salt adds a bit of complexity without overwhelming the other flavors. Because bark is essentially one big slab of chocolate, it can be a little bit tricky to temper. (Bark takes a long time to firm up and therefore has more opportunity to come out of temper or absorb ambient moisture, and its wide surface area is more likely to show streaks if it doesn't set up perfectly.) But no matter what, it is always delicious. If you prefer milk chocolate, you can substitute that for the 60% called for in this recipe; just follow the chocolate tempering guide on page 126.

2½ cups whole unsalted almonds, toasted

28 ounces dark chocolate (preferably 60% cacao)

2 teaspoons fleur de sel or other flaky sea salt

 tip

Make sure the room you're cooking in is nice and dry when you're making bark; on hot, muggy days we set the air conditioning to high before we get started.

1. Coarsely chop ½ cup of the almonds into large chunks; set aside. Line a sheet pan with parchment paper. Temper the chocolate using any of the tempering techniques listed on page 126, then bring it back to working temperature. When the chocolate is ready, fold the 2 cups whole almonds into the chocolate. Pour the chocolate-almond mixture onto the parchment paper–lined sheet pan. Bang the pan firmly on the counter a few times to release any air bubbles and help the chocolate spread out until it's only about ⅓ inch thick.

2. Sprinkle the chopped almonds and the sea salt evenly over the bark, then set the tray aside in a cool, dry place to let the chocolate firm up. Once the bark is completely set, use your hands to break it into large chunks. ★

Make Ahead

The bark can be stored in an airtight container at room temperature, in a single layer, for a month or longer.

 tip

Banging the tray of melted chocolate on the counter is preferable to tilting the tray or using a spatula to spread out the chocolate because it allows less opportunity for the chocolate to move around and break temper.

the marshmallow mixture will have cooled almost to room temperature and nearly quadrupled in volume. Remove the bowl and finish mixing by hand, using a rubber spatula in a beating motion and scraping down the sides and bottom of the bowl to ensure that all the cocoa is incorporated and no visible streaks remain.

5. To make cut marshmallows, pour the marshmallow mixture onto the prepared sheet pan and let it settle into a thick circle. Let the marshmallow cool for 5 minutes, then use a fine-mesh sieve to coat the top with a fine layer of cornstarch. Wrap the entire sheet pan in two layers of plastic wrap and set it aside to firm up overnight. When the marshmallows are firm, cut them into 1½-inch squares and toss them in cornstarch so they won't stick. Alternatively, to make piped marshmallows, transfer the marshmallow mixture to a pastry bag and pipe the marshmallows onto the desired surface. When the marshmallows are finished, let them sit for at least 20 minutes to firm up. ★

Make Ahead
The finished marshmallows will keep in an airtight container at room temperature for up to 2 weeks. If they become sticky, toss them in cornstarch.

When cutting marshmallows, dip your knife into hot water and wipe it dry between each cut to heat the metal.

Above and Beyond
Spiced Marshmallows
Substitute 1 tablespoon ground cinnamon or 1 to 2 teaspoons of stronger spices like nutmeg or cardamom for the cocoa powder. ★

Rocky Road

Makes about 15 squares

Rocky Road candy bars—a sweet, sticky combination of marshmallow, nuts, and chocolate—have been around since the early twentieth century, but the treat's exact origins are murky. The Annabelle Candy Company, makers of the Rocky Road candy bar, claims that its founder, Sam Altshuler, invented them, but Dreyer's Ice Cream and Fentons Creamery also claim to have made the original candy to mix into their ice creams. Our version was created as a way to use up the marshmallow "scraps" that were left over after we had cut our homemade marshmallows into even squares. The marshmallow is mixed with peanuts and 55% chocolate to give the whole thing a classic candy bar flavor, and cocoa nibs are added for extra crunch.

1½ quarts plain marshmallow (from the Chocolate Marshmallow recipe, without the cocoa added, page 141), very lightly packed

1½ cups roasted unsalted peanuts

⅓ cup cocoa nibs

20 ounces dark chocolate (preferably 55% cacao)

1. Cut or tear the marshmallows into rough squares 1 to 2 inches across. In a large bowl, combine the marshmallows, peanuts, and cocoa nibs, mixing the ingredients with your hands until they are well distributed.

2. Temper the chocolate using any of the tempering techniques listed on page 126, then bring it back to working temperature. When the chocolate is ready, add it to the bowl with the marshmallow mixture and mix everything well with a rubber spatula, making sure to scrape the bottom of the bowl and break up the bits of marshmallow so the chocolate coats everything as thoroughly as possible.

3. Line a sheet pan with parchment paper and pour the Rocky Road mixture onto the pan, leaving it piled up in a mound 1 to 1½ inches thick. Set it aside in a cool, dry place to set. Once the chocolate is fully set and firm to the touch, remove the confection from the parchment paper and cut it into 2- to 3-inch squares. ★

Make Ahead
The uncut slab of Rocky Road can be stored in an airtight container at room temperature for up to 1 month. Once it has been cut, it can be wrapped tightly in two layers of plastic wrap and kept at room temperature for up to 1 week.

This recipe works best when you make the marshmallows a couple of days ahead of time so they have time to dry out as much as possible. If they are freshly made or quite moist and stick together, you can set them out on a sheet pan to dry out for a couple of hours. Alternatively, you can toss them with a couple pinches of cornstarch and then shake out the excess in a sieve, but too much cornstarch can make the finished chocolate appear cloudy.

Chocolate Caramel Matzo

Makes 1 sheet pan of matzo

This Passover treat is addictively delicious. A simple combination of matzo covered with layers of rich caramel and semisweet chocolate and sprinkled with sea salt, it is crunchy, rich, sweet, and salty all at once. Our customers are always excited to see it appear on our shelves every year, and Naomi takes a huge helping of it to her aunt and uncle's house in Brooklyn for the family Seder. In the past we've sometimes made this recipe with walnuts instead of sea salt; both options are delicious, but we like how the sea salt in this version not only provides a nice contrast to the sweetness of the caramel but also echoes the Passover ritual of dipping foods into salty water.

4 or 5 matzo sheets

1½ cups granulated sugar

½ cup water

2 tablespoons plus 2 teaspoons light corn syrup

6 tablespoons (¾ stick) unsalted butter, cut into ½-inch slices

½ teaspoon baking soda

½ teaspoon salt

20 ounces dark chocolate (preferably 60% cacao)

1 tablespoon fleur de sel

When we make this recipe at The Chocolate Room, we make sure we have an extra person to help out—that way one person can start spreading the caramel out over the matzo while the other one is pouring it on.

recipe continues on the next page

1. Lay the matzo on a sheet pan in a single layer, breaking up one or two of the pieces if necessary so that they will all fit and fill the pan.

2. In a medium-large saucepan, combine the sugar, water, and corn syrup. Use a wet paper towel to wipe down the sides of the pot and have a cup of water with a pastry brush nearby. Bring the mixture to a vigorous boil over high heat. If sugar crystals form on the sides of the pan, brush them down with the wet pastry brush. When the sugar syrup begins to take on a golden hue around the edges, turn the heat to medium-low so that it doesn't cook too quickly, and continue boiling it, gently shaking and swirling the pot frequently to distribute the cooked sugar, until the caramel has a dark golden color, then immediately remove from the heat. Add the butter, baking soda, and salt, standing back from the pot to avoid the steam that will erupt from the addition of cool butter to hot sugar. Stir in the butter until it is fully melted and evenly distributed and the caramel has taken on an orange hue.

3. Pour the caramel onto the matzo, working from one end of the sheet pan to the other, and use a large offset spatula or a rubber spatula to spread it out so it covers all the matzo. (It's best to pour the caramel with one hand and start spreading the caramel with the other so that it doesn't cool down and firm up before you're finished.) Let the caramel cool to room temperature.

4. When the caramel has cooled, temper the chocolate using any of the tempering techniques listed on page 126, then bring it back to working temperature. When the chocolate is ready, pour it onto the caramel-covered matzo and spread it out with a small offset spatula or rubber spatula, covering as much of the caramel as possible.

5. Sprinkle the fleur de sel on top of the chocolate, then set the pan aside in a cool, dry place to let the chocolate firm up. Once the chocolate is completely set, use your hands to break the matzo into large chunks. ★

Make Ahead
The finished matzo will keep in an airtight container at room temperature for up to 5 days.

....

Make sure the caramel has cooled completely before covering it with the chocolate, or the steam from the cooling caramel will keep the tempered chocolate from setting properly.

....

**Contruction
Instructions**

S'mores
Makes about 36 s'mores

Make Ahead
The s'mores will keep in an
airtight container at room
temperature for 2 to 3 weeks.

Follow the instructions to make **¼ recipe Graham Cracker dough** (page 82). Cut and bake the graham crackers, but cut the crackers into 1-inch squares. Bake for 15 minutes and let cool to room temperature.

Follow the recipe for making **¼ recipe Marshmallow base** (page 141), but do not add the cocoa to the mixture and do not spread the mixture on sheet pans. While the mixture is still warm, use a rubber spatula to scoop the marshmallow base into a pastry bag fitted with a star tip, then let it sit to firm up for 10 minutes. (To see if it's ready to use, pipe a little of the marshmallow onto a paper towel or piece of parchment paper and see if it holds its shape.)

While the marshmallow mixture is setting, place **¼ cup Caramel Sauce** (page 162) in a squeeze bottle.

1

Squeeze a dime-size circle of caramel sauce onto each graham cracker.

2

Pipe a dollop of marshmallow onto each cracker, holding the star tip close to the cracker so the soft marshmallow base spreads out until it's close to the cracker's edges and then pulling it up so that it forms a conelike shape. (You should have a little over 1 tablespoon of marshmallow on each cracker.) When all the crackers have been topped with marshmallow, set them aside to firm up for 1 hour.

3

When the marshmallows are firm, temper **16 ounces dark chocolate** (preferably 60% cacao) using any of the tempering techniques listed on page 126, then bring it back to working temperature. When the chocolate is ready, drop a marshmallow-topped cracker into the chocolate and use a fork to scoop it out. Tap the fork on the edge of the bowl a couple dozen times to remove a lot of the chocolate, until there is only a thin layer and you can see the shape of the marshmallow through it. (If you need to, you can use a second fork to gently roll the confection in the chocolate.) Set the covered s'more on a parchment paper–lined sheet pan to firm up, and repeat with the rest of the crackers.

Hot Chocolate with White Marshmallow
recipes on pages 154 and 141

drinks
&
accompaniments

Tips & Tricks

How to Plate like The Chocolate Room

There's no real "right" way to serve the cakes, cookies, pies, and puddings we make at The Chocolate Room. Each dessert will be delicious paired with any of our sauces or ice creams or simply served on its own. That said, if you want to re-create the look and flavor of the desserts exactly the way you've had them in our cafés, here are a few tips that we follow—and a few tricks we use when we plate them up.

Tips

Portion Size

At The Chocolate Room, we like balance in our desserts. We don't want to taste too much of any one item on the plate, and, most important, we want guests to leave our cafés feeling satisfied but not overstuffed. When we serve our desserts, we portion everything so that there's just enough on the plate to fill you up without making you feel like you've had too much.

Toppings

Whenever we serve a topping on a dessert—whether it's a sauce or a spoonful of crunchy cocoa nibs—we always put half of the "topping" on the bottom of the dessert so that you can have some with every bite.

Cutting Cake

To cut perfect slices of cake with nice, clean edges, we always heat our knives by running them under hot water and drying them with a paper towel. If you're cutting more than once slice of cake at a time, you should reheat the knife after every slice.

Ice Cream Serving Size

When we serve scoops of ice cream as individual desserts—or when the ice cream is an integral part of a dessert, like it is in our Brownie Sundae (page 87)—we always instruct our staff to make a scoop just smaller than the size of a tennis ball, about 2½ inches in diameter. We think this is the perfect amount of ice cream; it's a generous amount but not so much that it's overwhelming.

Chocolate Shavings

We use a rotary cheese grater—the kind with a round barrel—to grate chocolate shavings to sprinkle onto our whipped cream. This design lets us store the chocolate right in the grater and also gives us the ability to grate the chocolate first, then tap the shavings out onto the dessert right where we want them.

Holding Ice Cream in Place

Whenever we serve a scoop of ice cream as an accompaniment to another dessert, we always put a small spoonful of chopped nuts or jagged cocoa nibs on the plate first, and nestle the ice cream into them to keep it from sliding around.

Plating Cake

When we cut a slice of cake, we let the slice fall onto the palm of our (gloved) hand, then we invert a serving plate on top of the cake and flip the two together. This way the slice won't fall apart as we flip it, and we can control how it's positioned on the plate.

Separating Hot and Cold

When we serve ice cream with both hot fudge (or caramel) and whipped cream, we always separate the hot and cold ingredients by pouring the sauce around the outside of the ice cream and putting the whipped cream on top of the scoop. This keeps the sauce from melting the whipped cream and causing it to slide off the top of the dessert.

Tricks

Dragging Sauce

When we serve sauce with a slice of cake or a piece of pie, we usually use this technique to spread it across the plate:

Put a pool of sauce, a little more than 1 tablespoon's worth, on one side of the plate.

Put the side edge of a spoon into the sauce and drag about two-thirds of the sauce across the plate.

Sauce Hearts

For special occasions (like proposals, anniversaries, and Valentine's Day), we use two sauces to make a heartlike design along the edges of a round dessert plate:

Using two squeeze bottles full of sauces with contrasting colors (like Raspberry Sauce and Chocolate Syrup), put alternating dots of sauce around the edge of the plate; the dots should barely touch each other. (For efficiency's sake, you can make all the dots of one sauce first, then do the second sauce.)

Use the tip of a paring knife or a toothpick to make a drag mark through the center of the all the dots; try to make the drag mark through all of the dots in one fluid motion. This will drag a little bit of each dot of sauce into the dot next to it, forming a heartlike shape.

Quenelles

When we serve whipped cream with our desserts, we use a hot spoon to shape it into a quenelle, an oblong shape popular in French cooking:

Put the whipped cream into a container with a wide mouth; ideally the top of the whipped cream will be near the top of the container.

Heat a long, narrow soup spoon in hot water, then dry it thoroughly.

Holding the spoon horizontally, dip the side of the spoon into the whipped cream until the bowl of the spoon is nearly submerged.

Pull the spoon toward you, through the whipped cream. The heat of the spoon will melt the cream just a little bit, and the cream will roll away from the spoon, forming an oblong dollop of cream. Scrape the quenelle along the side of the container so that it comes free from the rest of the whipped cream.

Not-Hots

These cool, creamy drinks are our homage to the famous Frrrozen Hot Chocolate from Serendipity 3, the dessert emporium on Manhattan's Upper East Side, near where we lived and worked when we were first dating.

Milk Chocolate Not-Hot

Makes 10 servings

4 cups whole milk

1 cup heavy cream

⅔ cup granulated sugar

½ cup unsweetened Dutch-process cocoa powder

16 ounces milk chocolate, coarsely chopped

4 teaspoons pure vanilla extract

Dark Chocolate Not-Hot

Makes 14 servings

6 cups whole milk

2 cups heavy cream

1 cup granulated sugar

1½ cups unsweetened Dutch-process cocoa powder

20 ounces dark chocolate (preferably 60% cacao), coarsely chopped

Crushed ice

Vanilla Whipped Cream (page 160)

Chocolate shavings (page 150)

1. In a medium saucepan, heat the milk, cream, and sugar until the liquid begins to steam, stirring occasionally to make sure the sugar doesn't stick to the bottom of the pan. Remove from the heat, add the cocoa powder, and whisk to dissolve. Add the chocolate and let it melt, about 5 minutes. If making the Milk Chocolate Not-Hot, add the vanilla.

2. Whisk until the chocolate and the liquid are fully combined. Pour the mixture into a heatproof storage container and refrigerate until it is very cold, at least 2 hours.

3. When you're ready to serve, for each glass of Not-Hot, put ¾ cup of the chocolate base and 1¾ cups crushed ice into a blender. Blend on medium speed until the drink has a slushy texture. Serve the Not-Hot in a tall glass and top with whipped cream and chocolate shavings. ★

Make Ahead
The Not-Hot bases can be kept in the refrigerator for 4 to 5 days.

Hot Chocolate—Three Ways

At The Chocolate Room we serve three different versions of our hot chocolate. We have a "classic" cocoa, which is made with a combination of cocoa and melted milk chocolate and is like a grown-up version of the hot cocoas we loved as children. We also make a dark cocoa, which is rich and intense, and a spiced dark cocoa made with ancho and chipotle chiles, cloves, and cinnamon. We serve the spiced cocoa at the Brooklyn Botanic Garden's Chile Pepper Festival every year, and attendees love it so much that many people come back for fourth and fifth servings. Pictured on page 148.

Classic Hot Chocolate Mix

Makes about 12 servings

¾ cup plus 2 tablespoons granulated sugar

1 cup unsweetened Dutch-process cocoa powder

12 ounces milk chocolate, coarsely chopped

Dark Hot Chocolate Mix

Makes about 12 servings

¾ cup sugar

1½ cups unsweetened Dutch-process cocoa powder

20 ounces dark chocolate (preferably 60% cacao), coarsely chopped

Spiced Dark Hot Chocolate Mix

Makes about 10 servings

½ cup plus 2 tablespoons granulated sugar

¾ cup plus 2 tablespoons unsweetened Dutch-process cocoa powder

1½ tablespoons ancho chile powder

2 teaspoons ground cinnamon

¼ teaspoon ground cloves

¼ teaspoon chipotle chile powder

13 ounces dark chocolate (preferably 60% cacao), coarsely chopped

1. Place the ingredients in a food processor and pulse repeatedly until everything is mixed together into a coarse powder and any remaining chunks of chocolate are no bigger than lentils. Don't let the machine run for more than a few seconds at a time or you might heat up the chocolate and cause it to melt, which will turn the powder into paste.

2. To use the powdered cocoa mixes, heat 1 cup milk or ¾ cup milk and ¼ cup water until steaming, then slowly whisk in ¼ cup of the cocoa mix. (For the Classic Hot Chocolate, you can also add about ⅛ teaspoon pure vanilla extract to the heated milk.) ★

Make Ahead
The cocoa mixes can be stored in airtight containers at room temperature for up to 3 months.

When the weather is cold we like to make a huge pot of these cocoas and have them ready to serve. To make these cocoas for a crowd, heat 10 or 12 servings milk in a stockpot until it begins to steam, whisk in the sugar, cocoa powder, and spices (if applicable), then turn off the heat before adding the chocolate; when the chocolate has melted, whisk and serve.

When we make the Classic Hot Chocolate in our cafés, we use an immersion blender to blend it up with the milk. We find this gives it the frothy quality of the cocoas we used to get from automatic cocoa dispensers when we were kids.

Chocolate Egg Cream

Makes 1 serving

When we developed the recipe for this classic New York treat, we consulted Naomi's uncle Howard Wasserman, a Brooklyn native who grew up helping out at his dad's luncheonette. Uncle Howard told us that to get the consistency of this drink right, it's important to mix the chocolate syrup and the milk together before you add the soda and that you should let the seltzer hit the back of the spoon as you add it to minimize the fizz.

2 tablespoons Chocolate Syrup (page 162)

½ cup whole milk

½ cup plus 2 tablespoons seltzer

 tip

Because this drink isn't served with ice, make sure the milk and seltzer are very cold before you mix everything together.

Using a long-handled spoon, mix the chocolate syrup and milk together in a tall, 10-ounce glass. Pour in the seltzer, allowing the stream of soda to hit the back of the spoon and stopping to stir a couple of times as you go. ★

Chocolate Sorbet

Makes about 4 pints

If you visit The Chocolate Room during the summer, this sorbet is the very first thing that you'll taste. It's as decadent as a sorbet can get, with almost as much melted chocolate as water. We serve it as an amuse-bouche, sometimes scooping hundreds of tiny spheres of it in a single night, and it's such a favorite that we wouldn't consider starting summer service with anything else. Make sure your ice cream machine is very, very cold so that you get a nice smooth texture.

5 cups water

1½ cups granulated sugar

¼ teaspoon salt

½ cup unsweetened Dutch-process cocoa powder

12½ ounces dark chocolate (preferably 60% cacao), coarsely chopped

4 teaspoons pure vanilla extract

Special Tool

Ice cream maker

1. In a large saucepan, combine the water, sugar, and salt, and cook over high heat, stirring occasionally, until the sugar has melted and the mixture is steaming vigorously and looks like it's about to come to a boil. Without turning off the heat, add the cocoa powder a little at a time, whisking well to break up any clumps. Remove from the heat, add the dark chocolate, and let it melt, about 1 minute. Add the vanilla and whisk well to combine. Refrigerate the sorbet base overnight.

2. Whisk the sorbet base well so the chocolate is evenly distributed, then transfer it to an ice cream maker and process according to the manufacturer's instructions. Transfer the sorbet to a container with a lid and freeze for at least 2 hours to firm up. ★

Chocolate Ice Cream

Makes about 3 pints

This decadent recipe is a little bit different from most ice cream recipes because it uses lots of rich melted chocolate. To offset the heaviness of the chocolate, we use both egg yolks, which are traditional in ice cream recipes, and a couple of whole eggs, which are more unusual; the added egg whites keep the mixture from being too dense and fudgy.

2½ cups whole milk

1 cup plus 2 tablespoons heavy cream

¾ cup plus 2 tablespoons granulated sugar

6 extra-large egg yolks

1 extra-large egg

¼ cup unsweetened Dutch-process cocoa powder

6 ounces dark chocolate (preferably 55% cacao), coarsely chopped

Special Tool

Ice cream maker

1. In a medium saucepan, combine the milk, cream, and ¾ cup of the sugar. Cook over medium-high heat, stirring occasionally, until the mixture begins to steam.

2. Meanwhile, in the bowl of a stand mixer fitted with the whisk attachment, whip the egg yolks, whole eggs, and the remaining 2 tablespoons sugar on high until the eggs are pale and form ribbons, about 2 minutes. Use a rubber spatula to scrape down the sides and bottom of the bowl, then whisk again for a few seconds until well combined.

3. When the dairy has started to steam, add the cocoa powder a little at a time, whisking well to break up any clumps. Cook until the mixture just comes to a rolling boil, then remove from the heat. With the mixer on medium-high, pour about 3 cups of the hot milk mixture into the eggs in a slow, steady stream to temper the eggs. Turn off the mixer and pour the tempered egg mixture back into the pan with the remaining milk mixture, whisking briskly.

5. Add the chocolate to the pot and let it melt, about 5 minutes, then whisk well to combine. Strain the ice cream base through a fine-mesh sieve into a bowl and let cool. Refrigerate the base overnight.

6. Before churning, whisk the ice cream base well so the chocolate is evenly distributed, then transfer to an ice cream maker and process according to the manufacturer's instructions. Transfer to a container with a lid and freeze for at least 2 hours to firm up. ★

Vanilla Ice Cream

Makes about 2 pints

This creamy ice cream, flavored with strong, rich Bourbon vanilla beans from Madagascar, is the perfect accompaniment for any chocolate dessert. It adds a cool, rich flavor to our chocolate cake à la mode, contrasts wonderfully with a heated brownie in our Brownie Sundae (page 87), and is the perfect canvas for rich hot fudge. With this ice cream—and with all our ice creams—we deviate a little from standard ice cream–making techniques in one key way: once we add the hot milk mixture to the egg yolks, we don't bother to continue to cook and thicken up the mixture. Our ice creams are just as rich and delicious without the extra cooking—not to mention quicker and easier to make.

1 cup whole milk

1 cup heavy cream

½ teaspoon pure vanilla extract

½ cup granulated sugar

½ vanilla bean (ideally Bourbon vanilla from Madagascar)

6 extra-large egg yolks

Special Tool

Ice cream maker

1. In a medium saucepan, combine the milk, cream, vanilla, and ¼ cup of the sugar. Split the vanilla bean in half lengthwise, use the back of the knife to scrape out the seeds, and then add both the seeds and the pod to the pan with the milk mixture. Cook over medium-high heat until the mixture just comes to a rolling boil, stirring occasionally.

2. Meanwhile, in the bowl of a stand mixer fitted with the whisk attachment, whip the egg yolks and remaining ¼ cup sugar on high until the yolks are pale and form ribbons, about 2 minutes. Use a rubber spatula to scrape down the sides and bottom of the bowl and then whip for a few seconds until well combined.

3. When the milk mixture has just come to a rolling boil, remove from the heat. With the mixer on medium-high, pour about 1 cup of the hot milk mixture into the eggs in a slow, steady stream to temper the eggs. Turn off the mixer and pour the tempered egg mixture into the pan with the remaining milk mixture, whisking briskly. Strain the ice cream base through a fine-mesh sieve into a bowl and let cool. Refrigerate the base overnight.

4. Transfer the chilled ice cream base to an ice cream maker and process according to the manufacturer's instructions. Transfer the ice cream to a container with a lid and freeze for at least 2 hours to firm up. ★

Strawberry Ice Cream

Makes about 3 pints

This bright, fruit-filled ice cream is a regular item in our ice cream case and an important component of our wonderful Banana Split (page 166). It's also excellent on its own with just a drizzle of hot fudge.

1½ cups whole milk

2½ cups heavy cream

1¼ cups granulated sugar

1 vanilla bean

9 extra-large egg yolks

2 cups hulled fresh or frozen strawberries

Special Tool

Ice cream maker

1. In a medium saucepan, combine the milk, cream, and ¾ cup of the sugar. Cut the vanilla bean in half lengthwise, use the back of the knife to scrape out the seeds, and then add both the seeds and the pod to the pan with the milk mixture. Cook over medium-high heat until the mixture just comes to a rolling boil.

2. Meanwhile, in the bowl of a stand mixer fitted with the whisk attachment, whip the egg yolks and ¼ cup of the sugar on high until the yolks are pale and form ribbons, about 2 minutes. Use a rubber spatula to scrape down the sides and bottom of the bowl and then whisk for a few seconds until well combined.

3. When the milk mixture has just come to a rolling boil, remove from the heat. With the mixer on medium-high, pour about 1½ cups of the hot milk mixture into the eggs in a slow, steady stream to temper the eggs. Turn off the mixer and pour the tempered egg mixture into the pan with the remaining milk mixture, whisking briskly. Strain the ice cream base through a fine-mesh sieve into a bowl and let cool to room temperature.

4. In a large bowl, combine the strawberries and the remaining ¼ cup sugar. Refrigerate the ice cream base and the strawberries overnight.

5. When the ice cream base has chilled, use an immersion or countertop blender to mash and puree the berries into small pieces, then stir them into the ice cream base. Transfer the chilled base to an ice cream maker and process according to the manufacturer's instructions. Transfer the ice cream to a container with a lid and freeze for at least 2 hours to firm up. ★

Mint Chip Ice Cream

Makes about 3 pints

Just one bite of this amazing ice cream is enough to make everyone who tries it fall in love with it. (In fact, Adam Richman, the host of TV's *Man v. Food*, once said it was one of the best things he'd ever eaten.) The thing that makes this recipe so special is that instead of using a flavoring or an extract, we use fresh mint in this ice cream, which gives it an almost surprisingly light, fresh flavor. And instead of adding regular chocolate chips, we drizzle thin streams of melted dark chocolate directly onto the ice cream; this way, each time you scoop some ice cream out of the tub, you break the chocolate into delicate little shards.

½ cup tightly packed fresh mint, torn into small pieces by hand

1 cup granulated sugar

3 cups whole milk

1 cup heavy cream

12 extra-large egg yolks

6 ounces dark chocolate (preferably 70% cacao), coarsely chopped

Special Tool

Ice cream maker

 tip

Mint stems have just as much flavor as the leaves, so both can be used in this recipe; make sure to cut off any dry or blackened leaves and ends because the black color will tint the milk and darken the ice cream.

1. In a large saucepan, combine the mint and ½ cup of the sugar. Smash and muddle the mint and sugar together with a wooden spoon until the mint is thoroughly bruised and the sugar has taken on enough moisture that it looks like slightly wet sand. Add the milk and cream and cook over medium-high heat until the mixture comes to a boil, stirring occasionally. When it has come to a boil, remove from the heat and let steep for at least 20 minutes.

2. Strain the mixture through a fine-mesh sieve into a bowl, pressing on the mint with a rubber spatula to make sure you're extracting all the flavorful liquid, then return the infused milk mixture to the pan and bring it to a boil over medium-high heat.

3. Meanwhile, in the bowl of a stand mixer fitted with the whisk attachment, whip the egg yolks and the remaining ½ cup sugar on high until the yolks are a little bit pale and form ribbons, about

2 minutes. Use a rubber spatula to scrape down the sides and bottom of the bowl and then whisk for a few seconds until well combined.

4. With the mixer on medium-high, pour about 3 cups of the hot milk mixture into the eggs in a slow, steady stream to temper the eggs. Turn off the mixer and pour the tempered egg mixture into the pan with the remaining milk mixture, whisking briskly.

5. Strain the ice cream base through a fine-mesh sieve into a bowl and let cool, then refrigerate overnight.

6. Transfer the chilled ice cream base to an ice cream maker and process according to the manufacturer's instructions.

continued on the next page

7. While the ice cream is churning, melt the chocolate in the top of a double boiler, stirring to keep it from burning, or microwave it in 30-second intervals, stirring after each interval, until it becomes liquid.

8. When the ice cream has churned, pour one-third of the still-soft ice cream into a wide casserole dish and smooth it out with a rubber spatula to form an even layer. Pour the chocolate into a plastic squeeze bottle or a pastry bag fitted with a very small tip and drizzle the melted chocolate over the ice cream layer in a zigzag pattern, first going up and down and then side to side; you should end up using about a third of the melted chocolate. Freeze the chocolate-covered ice cream for a couple of minutes to let the chocolate firm up, then repeat this procedure two more times, layering the ice cream and the drizzled chocolate on top of each other in the casserole dish. Freeze the ice cream until it's firm, 2 to 3 hours, then transfer it to storage containers. ★

Vanilla Whipped Cream

Makes 2 cups

We use this topping on everything from our Banana Cream Pie (page 99) to our Hot Chocolates (page 154). When we make whipped cream in our cafés, we mix the ingredients together and then store the flavored cream in tall metal containers, filled only half full, so that we can use an immersion blender to whip the cream right in the container whenever we need it.

2 cups heavy cream

1½ teaspoons pure vanilla extract

1½ tablespoons granulated sugar

Mix all the ingredients together in a large bowl or storage container and refrigerate. Just before serving, whip the flavored cream using an immersion blender on medium until it holds firm peaks. ★

Make Ahead
You can store the whipped cream in the refrigerator for 1 to 2 days, but some of it will turn to liquid at the bottom of the container. Rewhip the cream a bit just before serving, but be careful not to overwhip or it will have a grainy texture.

Above and Beyond
Vanilla Bean Whipped Cream
In a medium saucepan, heat 2 cups heavy cream with half a vanilla bean (seeds and pod, scraped) until it is steaming, then remove from the heat and let the mixture cool to room temperature. Whisk in 1½ tablespoons confectioners' sugar, then strain the mixture through a fine-mesh sieve. Refrigerate at least 2 hours. Whip the mixture as instructed above. ★

Hot Fudge

Makes 4 cups

When Jon was growing up, his go-to dessert was a hot fudge sundae, so we're very particular about our fudge. We think a great hot fudge should be thin enough to drizzle nicely but thick enough that it doesn't fall off a scoop of ice cream. It should also develop a nice chewy texture as it cools. We think our version hits all the marks and has a deep, rich cocoa flavor with a touch of saltiness to boot. Because the chocolate flavor in hot fudge comes exclusively from cocoa powder, it's important to use a high-quality cocoa—the better the cocoa is, the tastier the fudge will be.

1¼ cups heavy cream

1 cup (2 sticks) unsalted butter

½ teaspoon salt

1 cup granulated sugar

1 cup dark brown sugar

1¼ cups unsweetened Dutch-process cocoa powder

In a medium saucepan, combine the cream, butter, and salt and cook over medium-high heat until the butter has melted. Reduce the heat to medium-low and add both sugars. Cook, whisking occasionally, until the sugars have melted, then add the cocoa powder and whisk until it has dissolved. (The mixture should be thick, but if it starts to bubble along the edges, turn the heat down.) Remove from the heat and let the fudge cool for a couple of minutes, then blend with an immersion blender until the fudge is completely smooth; alternatively, let the mixture cool to body temperature and then blend it in a countertop blender. ★

Make Ahead
This recipe can be stored in the refrigerator for up to 2 weeks or canned in jam jars in a hot water bath (following the jar manufacturer's instructions). One recipe makes 4 (8-ounce) jars. (They make an excellent gift.) Reheat it in a hot water bath or in the microwave in 1-minute intervals, stirring after each interval so it doesn't burn.

Chocolate Syrup

Makes 2 cups

This rich, dark chocolate syrup is one of the most versatile items in our cafés. We use it in our Black-Bottom Butterscotch Custard (page 113), as an ice cream topping, as a garnish for amuse-bouches, to flavor our Chocolate Egg Cream (page 155), and for much, much more.

½ cup water

½ cup granulated sugar

⅓ cup light corn syrup

¼ teaspoon salt

8 ounces dark chocolate (preferably 60% cacao)

2¼ teaspoons pure vanilla extract

In a small saucepan, combine the water, sugar, corn syrup, and salt and cook over high heat, stirring occasionally. When the sugar has melted and the mixture is steaming, remove from the heat and add the chocolate. Let the mixture sit until the chocolate has melted, about 5 minutes. Whisk until the mixture is fully emulsified and has become a smooth sauce, then add the vanilla and whisk again briefly. Transfer the sauce to a heatproof storage container and let cool slightly. Cover and refrigerate until cold before using. ★

Make Ahead
The sauce can be stored in the refrigerator for up to 3 weeks. Reheat the sauce in a hot water bath or by microwaving it in 30-second intervals, stirring well after each interval to smooth out the texture of the sauce.

Caramel Sauce

Makes about 3 cups

We use this dark, flavorful caramel sauce in our Turtle Cheesecake (page 47) and our S'mores (page 146), and we add a drizzle of it to plated desserts like our Chocolate Chip Almond Cake (page 32). It also makes an excellent topping for ice cream and can be made in large batches and sealed in jars so that it is shelf stable and can be gifted to friends and family.

1½ cups heavy cream

½ vanilla bean (ideally Bourbon vanilla from Madagascar)

2¼ cups granulated sugar

½ cup water

2 tablespoons light corn syrup

4 tablespoons (½ stick) unsalted butter, cut into ½-inch slices

1. Put the cream in a medium saucepan. Split the vanilla bean in half lengthwise and scrape out the seeds. Add both the vanilla bean pod and seeds to the cream. Heat the cream over medium-high heat until it begins to steam, then remove from the heat, cover the pot, and let steep, making sure it stays warm.

2. In a large, tall-sided saucepan, combine the sugar, water, and corn syrup. Use a wet paper towel to wipe down the sides of the pot and have a cup of water with a pastry brush nearby. Bring the mixture to a vigorous boil over high heat. If sugar crystals form on the sides of the pan, brush them down with the wet pastry brush. Once the sugar mixture begins to take on a deep golden color, watch it carefully and swirl it a little if some areas are darkening faster than others. (Don't use a spoon to stir or the sugar might form crystals.) Wash down the sides of the pot as necessary to remove sugar crystals. Cook until the caramel takes on a deep amber color, then remove from the heat. (The mixture will begin to smell slightly of burnt sugar.)

3. Add the butter a piece or two at a time, being careful the mixture doesn't bubble up too much, and use a long-handled whisk to mix it into the caramel. Carefully add the warm cream, beginning with just a couple of tablespoons at a time and increasing as the mixture cools, whisking as you add it and making sure to stand back as the caramel bubbles up. Let the caramel settle between additions. When all the cream has been added, whisk gently to make sure the ingredients are well incorporated.

4. Strain the caramel through a fine-mesh sieve into a metal container and let cool to room temperature before storing it in the refrigerator or canning it in a hot water bath (see below). ★

Make Ahead
This sauce can be stored in the refrigerator for up to 2 weeks or canned in jam jars in a hot water bath (following the jar manufacturer's instructions). Reheat the sauce in a hot water bath or by microwaving it in 30-second intervals, stirring well after each interval to smooth out the texture of the sauce. If the caramel separates, mix it back together with a spoon.

When making caramel, crystallization around the edges of the pot doesn't pose a real problem unless the crystals start to build on each other and extend into the pot. If these crystals begin to form, you may be able to save the caramel by putting a tight-fitting lid on the pot so that condensation from the heat will run down the sides of the pot and wash the crystals back into the rest of the caramel.

Above and Beyond
Chocolate-Caramel Sauce
Combine equal parts Caramel Sauce and Chocolate Syrup (both facing page) and stir well to make a delicious chocolate-caramel sauce. ★

Strawberry Sauce

Makes 2 cups

This light, summery sauce is wonderful on any of our ice creams and is usually served on our classic banana split (page 166). We make this sauce with fresh or frozen fruit, depending on the season, and we add just a touch of balsamic vinegar to bring out the flavor of the berries.

1 pound hulled fresh or frozen strawberries
½ cup plus 2 tablespoons granulated sugar
½ cup water
¼ teaspoon salt
¼ teaspoon balsamic vinegar

1. In a medium saucepan, combine half of the strawberries, ½ cup of the sugar, and the water and cook over medium-high heat until the strawberries are warm (if using frozen strawberries, they should soften). Remove from the heat, add the salt, and use an immersion blender to puree the mixture into a smooth sauce. (Alternatively, you can wait for the berries to cool, then blend the mixture in a countertop blender.) Strain the mixture through a fine-mesh sieve, pressing it through with a rubber spatula or flexible pastry scraper, and discard the seeds and pulp.

2. Return the liquid to the pot, add the remaining strawberries and remaining 2 tablespoons sugar, and cook the mixture over medium heat until the strawberries are just warm and soft. Remove from the heat and use the immersion blender to break up the berries a little bit, but allow some chunks to remain. Add the vinegar and stir to combine; let the mixture cool to room temperature. ★

Make Ahead
This sauce will keep in the refrigerator for up to 1 week.

Raspberry Chambord Sauce

Makes 4 cups

Raspberry is one of our favorite flavors to pair with chocolate, and this bright, colorful sauce is used as an accompaniment for many desserts, especially our Single-Origin Flourless Chocolate Cake (page 38). It is also excellent on ice cream.

1 pound frozen raspberries, thawed

2 tablespoons plus 2 cups sugar

3 cups water

¼ cup raspberry liqueur, such as Chambord

¼ cup ruby port

Special Tool

Plastic ruler

1. In a blender, combine the raspberries and 2 tablespoons of the sugar and blend into a smooth puree. Strain the mixture through a fine-mesh sieve into a medium saucepan, pressing the ingredients through with a rubber spatula to remove the seeds. (Some of the seeds will escape through the sieve, but most will be removed from the sauce.)

2. Add the water, the remaining 2 cups sugar, and the raspberry liqueur to the pan with the puree and heat over medium heat until the sauce begins to bubble slightly. Use a plastic ruler to measure how deep the liquid is, then simmer the sauce, stirring occasionally, until it has reduced by one-third. Add the port and cook for 5 minutes more to cook off the alcohol. Remove from the heat and measure the sauce. If you have less than 4 cups of sauce, add water to make up the difference; if you have more, return the sauce to the pan and cook until it has further reduced. When the sauce is done, let it cool to room temperature and then refrigerate until cold. ★

Make Ahead
The sauce can be kept in the refrigerator for up to 10 days.

Peanut Butter Sauce

Makes about 3 cups

This fudgelike peanut butter sauce is incredibly simple to make and is wonderful on any kind of ice cream, particularly our classic Chocolate Ice Cream (page 156).

1 cup heavy cream

½ cup granulated sugar

½ cup light corn syrup

4 tablespoons (½ stick) unsalted butter

1 teaspoon pure vanilla extract

1½ cups natural creamy peanut butter with salt

1. In a medium-large saucepan, combine the cream, sugar, corn syrup, butter, and vanilla and cook over medium-high heat, whisking occasionally, until the butter has melted, the sugar has dissolved, and the mixture begins to bubble a bit. Remove from the heat and let the syrup cool to room temperature.

2. When the syrup has cooled, add the peanut butter and whisk until the sauce is smooth. ★

Make Ahead
This sauce can be kept in the refrigerator for up to 1 week.

Marshmallow Sauce

Makes about 2 cups

Sweet, gooey marshmallow sauce (or "fluff") was invented in 1917 in Somerville, Massachusetts, not too far from where Jon's grandfather ran an ice cream parlor a few decades later. We use this sauce in the filling for our Whoopie Pies (page 83) and on many of our ice cream sundaes. As with all our recipes that use uncooked egg whites, we use pasteurized eggs when we make this in the cafés.

1 extra-large egg white

½ cup light corn syrup

¾ teaspoon pure vanilla extract

½ cup confectioners' sugar

In the bowl of a stand mixer fitted with the whisk attachment, whip the egg white and corn syrup on high until the mixture is very fluffy and holds stiff peaks, about 3 minutes. Turn the mixer to medium-low, add the vanilla, then mix on high for a few seconds, until the vanilla has been fully incorporated. With the mixer on medium-low, slowly add the confectioners' sugar in three or four additions so that it doesn't fly out of the bowl. Turn the mixer back to high and whip until the sugar has been fully incorporated. Use a rubber spatula to scrape down the sides and bottom of the bowl and the whisk attachment, then whip again for a few seconds until well combined. The marshmallow sauce should be very sticky—you may need to use your fingers to remove it from the whisk. ★

Make Ahead
The marshmallow sauce can be kept in the refrigerator for 2 to 3 days.

Contruction Instructions

Banana Split

Makes 1 banana split

1 — Cut **1 unpeeled banana** in half lengthwise. Dust the cut side of each banana half with **1 teaspoon raw or granulated sugar** and use a kitchen torch to caramelize the sugar until is has a nice dark golden brown color. (Alternatively, caramelize the sugar under your oven's broiler.) Set the banana halves aside to cool. Once the sugar has hardened, peel the banana halves. Place the brûléed banana halves along the sides of a long ice cream dish, with the caramelized parts facing out.

2 — Place a large scoop of **Vanilla Ice Cream** (page 157) in the center of the dish. Place a large scoop of **Chocolate Ice Cream** (page 156) and **Strawberry Ice Cream** (page 158) on either side of the vanilla ice cream.

3 — Ladle about **2 tablespoons heated Hot Fudge** (page 161) onto the strawberry ice cream, **2 tablespoons heated Caramel Sauce** (page 162) onto the vanilla ice cream, and **2 tablespoons Strawberry Sauce** (page 163) onto the chocolate ice cream.

4 — Top each scoop of ice cream with **Vanilla Whipped Cream** (page 160) and dust the whipped cream with **chocolate shavings** (see page 150).

5 — Finish the whole thing off with **1 fresh, candied, or brandied cherry** on the middle dollop of whipped cream.

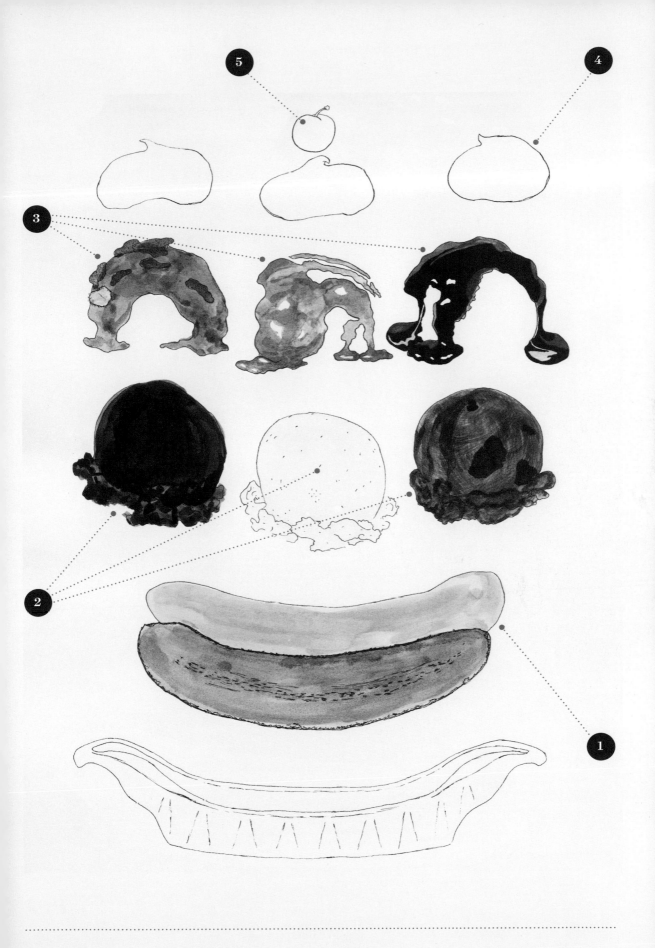

Mocha

2 tablespoons Chocolate Syrup (page 162) plus more for decoration

1 shot espresso

1 cup whole milk, steamed or heated

Foamed milk (optional)

Pour the syrup into the bottom of a mug, add the espresso, and stir to combine. Pour in the milk and top with foamed milk, if using. If using foamed milk, drizzle with additional chocolate syrup.

Café Lou

½ cup Dark Hot Chocolate (page 154)

½ cup brewed coffee, hot

Combine the ingredients in a large mug and stir.

Torino

5 ounces Dark Hot Chocolate (page 154)

1 shot espresso

Foamed milk (optional)

Combine the hot chocolate and the espresso. Top with the foamed milk, if using.

Chocolate Milk

3 tablespoons Chocolate Syrup (page 162)

1 cup whole milk

Combine in a blender or whisk thoroughly.

Hot Chocolate Float

5 ounces Dark Hot Chocolate (page 154)

1 scoop Vanilla Ice Cream (page 157)

Fill a mug three-quarters full with hot chocolate and add the ice cream.

Chocolate Ice Cream Shake

2 very large scoops of Chocolate Ice Cream (page 156), each about 3 inches in diameter

¾ cup whole milk

In a blender, process the ingredients on low until the mixture is smooth.

Cava Cocktail

1 ounce Raspberry Chambord Syrup (page 164) or Strawberry Sauce (page 163)

3 ounces cava (Spanish sparkling wine)

Pour the syrup into a 4-ounce champagne flute and fill the glass slowly with the cava, stirring as you pour.

Chocolate Stout Float

1 large scoop of Vanilla Ice Cream (page 157)

12 ounces chocolate beer (preferably Brooklyn Brewery Chocolate Stout)

Put the ice cream in the bottom of a 16-ounce glass and pour the beer over it.

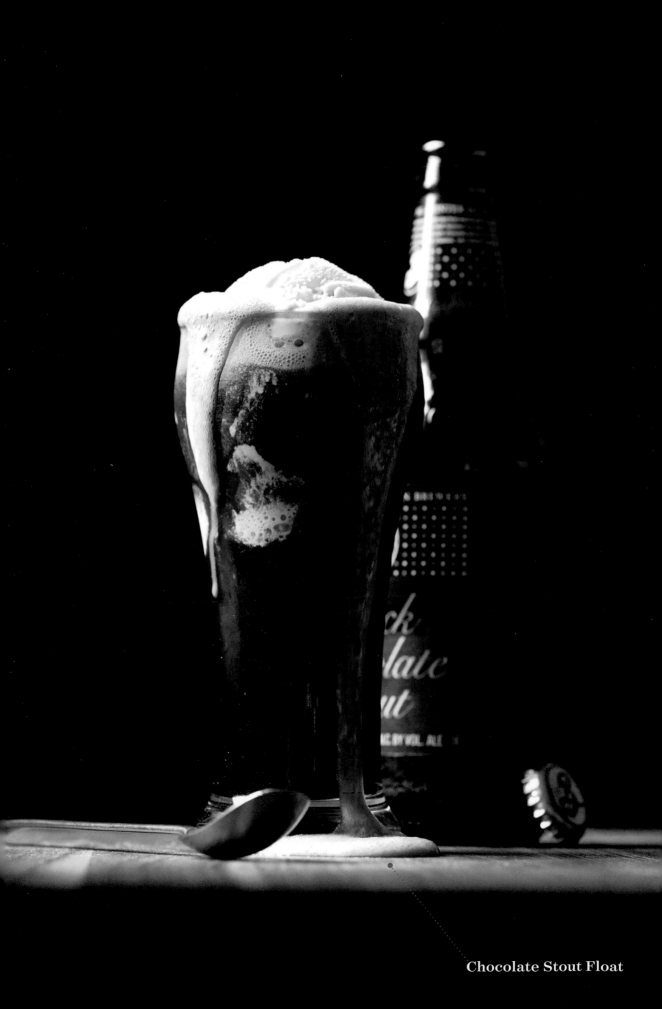

Chocolate Stout Float

Acknowledgments

We would like to thank the many people who worked on this book and supported us through its conception and creation. First and foremost, we would like to thank The Chocolate Room's executive pastry chef, Carmine Arroyo, our invaluable partner who worked tirelessly on this book, and whose palate, vision, and focus have helped make the business what it is today. Special thanks to Ariele Schwartz, for her positive attitude, organizational skills, pastry talents, and support on all fronts whenever and wherever we needed it, everyday, without question. We are very grateful to the many chefs of The Chocolate Room, past and present, whose ideas and hard work helped make this book possible, including Margaret Hastings, Sydney Jones, Jennifer Jupiter, Margaret Kyle, Lorelie Magampon, Amy Marsh, Katie Meehan, Elizabeth Ramsey Day, Amy O'Hare, Christina Trush, Rob Valencia, and Anastasia Weiss.

We greatly appreciate all the efforts of Georgia Freedman, who first pitched us the idea of this book project and then worked diligently to write all the text and see it through to completion. We are grateful for your attention to detail, collaborative spirit, and dedication to bring these recipes out of our kitchens, to be shared by all. Many thanks to the team that Rizzoli organized for this book, including our extraordinary editor, Christopher Steighner, for his gentle, creative, and open-minded attitude, enthusiasm, and dedication toward this project; photographer Ben Fink, illustrator Elizabeth Ashley, and stylist Maeve Sheridan for the gorgeous images that bring the recipes to life; designer Jennifer S. Muller for her beautiful vision for the book; and copy editor Ivy McFadden for her attention to detail. Many thanks as well to our agents, Carla Glasser and Sarah Lazin, who have been incredibly supportive throughout this entire process.

We would like to thank the staff who took time out of busy production schedules to help Georgia learn to make all of these recipes, and our small army of volunteer recipe testers, including Jill Bailard, Vered and Lena Ben-Gideon, Kaitlin Bruner, Caroline Buehring, Matthew Freedman, Ana Freire, Heather Isiminger, Hilary Jacks, Catherine Martin Christopher, Ashlyn Clark McCague, Allie Okner, Leslie Russell, Keto Shimizu, Barbara Wand, Katherine Weitkunat, and Emily Wolman; as well as Janyne Cooper, Andrew Kirschenbaum, Beth Kracklauer, Michael Krondl, Christopher Michael, Ben Mims, and Karen Shimizu for their assistance and support.

Thanks to our families for their endless support and patience throughout this process, especially Clare and Mae Payson, the Payson family, the Josepher family, Marlene and Howard Wasserman, Josh and Nora Freedman-Wand, Rendy Freedman, and Jerry Freedman.

Finally, we'd like to thank the people who have supported The Chocolate Room throughout its years in business, including Cara Mia Aiello, Vito and Josephine Balsamo, Leslie and Bill Bercume, Joan and Bob Bier, Mike and Shelley Boots, Mary Margaret Chapel, Chris Coppolillo, Peter Coppolillo, Armando Cruz, Dorothy Cullman, Joe Cullman, Lewis B. Cullman and Louise Hirschfield-Cullman, Lucy Danziger, Amanda Dunham, Dawn Fischer and Stacey Friedman, Freddy and Gladys Garrastegui, Joel Hamburger, Gary Holbrook, Barbara and Tom Israel, Robin Johnson, Brian Josepher, Herb Josepher, Susan Josepher, Ben Kleinman, Dan Kleinman, Sol Kleinman, Fritz Knipschildt, Lara and Stan Lai, Jeff Lederman, Elizabeth Maher, Louis Navaer, Ann and Peter Payson, Stephen Payson, Cass Robbins, Susan and Peter Solomon, Eleanor and Norman Solovay, Paul Takeuchi, Aaron Taylor-Walman, and Jeff Younger; the invaluable friends and customers who have supported us from our opening day; and our past and present employees for making The Chocolate Room the special place it is today.

Conversion Chart All conversions are approximate.

Liquid Conversions

U.S.	Metric
1 tsp	5 ml
1 tbsp	15 ml
2 tbsp	30 ml
3 tbsp	45 ml
¼ cup	60 ml
⅓ cup	75 ml
⅓ cup + 1 tbsp	90 ml
⅓ cup + 2 tbsp	100 ml
½ cup	120 ml
⅔ cup	150 ml
¾ cup	180 ml
¾ cup + 2 tbsp	200 ml
1 cup	240 ml
1 cup + 2 tbsp	275 ml
1¼ cups	300 ml
1⅓ cups	325 ml
1½ cups	350 ml
1⅔ cups	375 ml
1¾ cups	400 ml
1¾ cups + 2 tbsp	450 ml
2 cups (1 pint)	475 ml
2½ cups	600 ml
3 cups	720 ml
4 cups (1 quart)	945 ml
	(1,000 ml is 1 liter)

Weight Conversions

U.S./U.K.	Metric
½ oz	14 g
1 oz	28 g
1½ oz	43 g
2 oz	57 g
2½ oz	71 g
3 oz	85 g
3½ oz	100 g
4 oz	113 g
5 oz	142 g
6 oz	170 g
7 oz	200 g
8 oz	227 g
9 oz	255 g
10 oz	284 g
11 oz	312 g
12 oz	340 g
13 oz	368 g
14 oz	400 g
15 oz	425 g
1 lb	454 g

Oven Temperatures

°F	Gas Mark	°C
250	½	120
275	1	140
300	2	150
325	3	165
350	4	180
375	5	190
400	6	200
425	7	220
450	8	230
475	9	240
500	10	260
550	Broil	290

Naomi Josepher and **Jon Payson** founded The Chocolate Room, a sophisticated dessert café and retail shop. The couple operates two Brooklyn locations that have become destinations for chocolate lovers from all over.

Georgia Freedman is a food and travel writer living in the San Francisco Bay Area. She writes for *The Wall Street Journal*, *Lucky Peach*, *Saveur*, *Afar*, and *Zester Daily*, among other publications.